VOICES INTERN

P R

Sunny 101:

The 10 Commandments Of A Boss Chick

SUNSHINE SMITH-WILLIAMS

Sunny 101: The 10 Commandments of a Boss Chick

Sunny 101: The 10 Commandments of a Boss Chick is written as a self-help guide, based on the real-life experiences of Sunshine Smith-Williams. This book is designed as a tool to empower women and enlighten them to the consequences of poor choices. Although the stories the author shares about herself are true, the examples illustrated about others are false (except the life of Jamila T. Davis, which is excerpted from her memoirs). Any likeness to real-life people is merely a coincidence. The author created each scenario in the examples simply to illuminate the message in the text.

Printed in the United States of America
First Printing, 2015

Library of Congress Control Number: 2015931941
ISBN: 978-0-9911041-6-1
Voices International Publications
196-03 Linden Blvd.
St. Albans, NY 11412

"Changing Lives One Page at a Time."

www.voicesbooks.com

Cover Design by: Keith Saunders (www.mariondesigns.com)
Typesetting by: Jana Rade (www.impactstudioonline.com)
Edited by: Dr. Maxine Thompson and Alanna Boutin

DEDICATION

This book is dedicated to every woman, whether young or mature, who is willing to learn, acknowledge, and change their flaws, just as I did.

As you read, please do not judge yourselves harshly, but use the mirroring images from each chapter to modify your morals, values, and goals.

I want to also dedicate this book to my great-great-cousin, the renowned author Mr. Richard N. Wright (author of *Native Son*). Although we never met, you have always been an inspiration for me to write, as my grandmother Gladys Wright-Fleming shared incredible stories about your life journey. May your legacy forever live on!

ACKNOWLEDGMENTS

First, I want to thank Almighty God for giving me this gift and choosing me to deliver this message. I am grateful for the challenges and life experiences you have allowed me to endure. They have given me the strength and wisdom to write this book.

I extend my thanks to my sister from another mister and my writing muse, Ms. Jamila T. Davis, who helped me broaden my scope creatively. Without you I couldn't have completed this project. A special thank you to my editor, Dr. Maxine Thompson. You are truly a blessing sent at the right time! Thank you to Sean Craig and Catherine Floyd for helping me fine-tune this project. Your help is greatly appreciated. I thank my cousin, Minister Andrew Fleming, for the helpful spiritual references I needed to put this book together. And, thank you to my publisher, Voices International Publications, for believing in this project. I'm ready to take this to the top!

Last but not least, I want to thank my husband, who is truly my soul mate, for giving me the inspiration to keep going when I wanted to stop. I recognize the gift God has given me in you. Thank you for always being a team player! I love you.

TABLE OF CONTENTS

PROLOGUE

My S600 Mercedes-Benz felt like it was floating as I sped down the highway listening to Young Jeezy. The shots of Patrón I had earlier finally kicked in, and I was ready to turn up! Anxiously, I arrived at my destination. Placing my car in park, I quickly took off my Gucci thong sandals, grabbed my toe candy from the passenger floor, and began putting on my Je T'aime shoes. My knee-high python boots were everything!

I hopped out of my milky-white, high-end sedan and gave the key to the parking attendant. It had been awhile since I partied at Sue's Rendezvous, the notorious strip club in Westchester, New York, known for extravagant adult events and high-class celebrity appearances. It was the night I was celebrating the debut of my four-page spread in *Straight Stuntin* magazine. It was the magazine's 6-year anniversary edition, and I was honored to be the first and only female entrepreneur featured for having the combined talent of brains and beauty.

I entered the VIP section, making a grand appearance in my Swarovski crystal-studded, skintight, sheer Versailles jumpsuit, designed by Musa. Immediately, I joined my friend Slay, a well respected businessman and DJ in the hip-hop music industry, also the owner of *Straight Stuntin* magazine. Slay grabbed the mic and shouted me out. "What's good, Sunny Money Queens?!! You looking good, baby!"

For that moment all eyes were focused on me. I was the center of attention, and it felt extremely good! Bottles of champagne filled the VIP as we partied the night away with celebrities Fred the Godson, Kid Capri, Myson, and Jazzie Belle, along with other published models who were featured in the magazine. With a bottle of Moët in one hand and a rack of singles in the other hand I noticed a familiar face which I hadn't seen in a while.

"Oh look, my dude, E!" I shouted across the club.

I hadn't seen E in ages! After a picture of him surfaced on social media he stopped coming around the hood. E was in the closet but a few of us knew what time it was. He had a history of dealing with homely chicks for a hot plate and a roof over his head. E waved his hand eagerly to get my attention.

"Yo, Sunny Money, what's good? Help me get up in VIP," he shouted over the loud music.

"Yo, give me a second," I replied as I politicked with Slay to get E in.

Within seconds the bouncer let E into the crowded VIP area, and he gave me a big hug.

"Damn, I see you doing it, Ma. Don't hurt 'em!" E commented in a flamboyant manner. The lisp at the end of his sentence reminded me of the gay character Anton in the '90s comedy show *In Living Color.*

I didn't mind the fact that E was gay. What was important was he knew how to have a good time! From the moment he joined me in VIP, the energy in the atmosphere exploded, and we turned all the way up! Before I knew it, the lights were coming on and the party was over. I dreaded driving all the way back to Long Island to my empty minimansion. My husband Holiday was out of town on business, so I knew I'd be stuck cuddling up alone. As we exited the club I noticed E appeared disturbed.

"Yo, you straight?" I questioned taking note of his frazzled facial expression.

"Not really. Umm, I need a ride. Do you think you can take me to Queensbridge?" E asked scrolling through his iPhone 5.

"Well, umm, that's all the way in the other direction, but I guess I can. Give me a minute. Let me get some bottled water to avoid a hangover," I said thinking about how I had just committed myself to traveling 45 minutes away in the opposite direction. In my mind I rationalized it as okay. I was helping out an old friend, plus Holiday was away so I was going to be home alone. E was funny and energetic, so I knew the time would pass by quickly.

In the car ride to Queensbridge I learned E was headed to meet up with his daughter and his baby mother. Going to the strip club had distracted him from his prior obligations, but he made it clear that his daughter was a priority as he expressed his genuine love and admiration for her. For a moment he touched my heart by his dialogue. I couldn't help but to wish my deadbeat dad would have felt as compassionate about me. From that conversation I learned another side about E. He was sensitive and compassionate.

I pulled up to the Ravenwood Housing Project in Astoria, New York, and E hopped out.

"Sunny Money, give me a few minutes. I'll be right back," he said as he disappeared into the large housing project.

As I sat behind the wheel waiting for him to come back, I began to feel nauseated. All the champagne and Patrón I drank earlier was quickly catching up to me. I opened the door to vomit when E approached.

"Damn, Sunny Money, you can't handle your liquor," he said with laughter.

"No, I'm straight now. I just had to get it out of my system," I quickly replied, embarrassed that he caught me off guard.

"Listen, I have an issue, Ma. My baby's mother and my daughter left already, and I don't have a ride to get to them. Do you think you can take me upstate?" he asked leaning into my passenger-car window that was halfway down.

"Upstate? Yo, you bugging! Absolutely not! No, no, and hell no!" I replied quickly assembling myself, ready to ride off.

"Hold up, Sunny. Please! I'll pay you," E said as he took a stack of money out of his pocket.

"Whatever you want, Sunny, just tell me your price."

I stared at the money contemplating his proposition. I didn't need the cash, but I wasn't one to turn away easy money. Before I could settle my thoughts E began to count out hundred dollar bills.

"1-2-3-4-5-6-7-8-9-10. Here goes a stack, Ma," E said as he handed me the crisp Federal Reserve notes.

"Are we good?" he questioned.

"Well, I guess so, but you are gonna drive!" I said as I pulled off my Je T'aime shoes and climbed over to the passenger side of the vehicle.

"Deal!" E replied. He took the wheel, and we drove off.

I cuddled up in the passenger seat, turning on the heat and massage options, and quickly fell fast asleep. Several hours later, I was jilted out of my sleep by a loud noise.

Booooooooom!!!

INTRODUCTION

Allow me a moment to introduce myself to some and reacquaint with others. I am Sunshine Smith-Williams aka Sunny "Money" Queens, the official Boss Chick extraordinaire!!! My self-proclaimed title is not only validated by my experience and contributions to the game, but my accomplishments over the last 35 years radiate the depth of the power that resides in me. I not only know who I am, I have a clear understanding of who I belong to, and my obligations to Him, my Creator.

By His grace, today I am a successful author, manager, film producer, real estate broker, legal consultant, and co-owner of a thriving chain of shoe stores, Je T'aime Shoes. Along with these endeavors, I have managed to run several other profitable business ventures while maintaining my status as a caring mother to my 6-year-old son and being a loving wife. Nothing in life was handed to me; I had to work hard for everything I have. The struggles I've encountered and conquered have made me the woman that I am today, by definition . . . a true Boss Chick.

For those who believe we are all a product of our environment, I am here to prove you wrong! I grew up in some of the grittiest housing projects in Queens, New York. I can vividly remember stepping over fresh piss in the elevator and pushing past prostitutes and hustlers to get to school. Some nights I had difficulty sleeping due to my neighbors' police drug raids. I was told by many that I was destined to fail and would never make my way out of the projects. Plenty of haters attempted to make me their prey. Instead of allowing their negative energy to derail me, I used it as fuel to push my way to the top! It is my drive, my tenacity, and my ambition that certifies me as an ultimate Boss Chick!

As I took note of many women who share my struggles, pain, and dilemmas, I decided to write *The 10 Commandments of a Boss Chick* to provide a road map for women to avoid common pitfalls that derail us from achieving our dreams. I created this book for those like myself who have taken major hits in life, yet chose to excel. This book is written to motivate, inspire, and give you wisdom to push past adversity and empower you to embrace success.

Unlike many self-help books geared to reach today's generation, this book is written from a "hood" perspective. I don't dress up life's issues; I tell it like it is! My delivery may be a tad bit rough and raw, but it's real! I'm not here to claim I'm perfect or to profess that I've never made a mistake. Contrarily, I wrote this book to expose my flaws and to share many of the life lessons I've learned from my failures. I've been knocked down several times, yet these same experiences have molded me and prepared me for success. Most importantly, it taught me to recognize my self-worth, a gift I'd like to share with you!

This book is not written to cast judgment. However, it should be used as a mirror of reflection. Our stories may defer, but our struggles and pain will surely resemble! We may have been dealt a similar deck of cards, but it is not the cards that matter; it's how you play the game! When the odds are stacked against you, you will have to "G" up! Meaning, when you know that obstacles lie ahead, you have to plan to win or you will surely fail.

A Boss Chick is a woman who can acknowledge her mistakes and use them as a platform for greater success. She is a woman who never remains stagnant. She may fall short at times, but like a good football player, she strategizes a way out . . . and comes out on top! A Boss Chick makes "moves" and not "movies." Although confused admirers may try to dull her "crown" or discredit her, she will undoubtedly still be respected.

Life is about preference, discretion, and judgment. A Boss Chick knows what she wants, how she'll get it, and what to do when she achieves her goals. A Boss Chick is led by principles, morals, and values. She never allows today's possible gains impede her future success. A Boss Chick is ambitious, credible, confident, and courageous. The radiance of her character and beauty summons the attention of all others when she walks in a room. Most importantly, a Boss Chick commands RESPECT!

A Boss Chick is never threatened in the presence of others. She is not jealous of her sister's accomplishments. Instead, a Boss Chick sees her own reflection in her sister when she succeeds. She welcomes constructive criticism and takes heed to it. She never thinks she's too good to learn from anyone when the opportunity presents itself. A Boss Chick eats with her sisters, not competes with her sisters. She's smart enough to utilize all alliances to win!

In this book I offer my many years of experience in the hood, corporate board rooms, and personal relationships to give my sisters a road map to navigate what I learned "the hard way." Similar to manuals that men live by such as *The Art of War* by Sun Tzu and *The 50th Law,* written by my brother Curtis "50 Cent" Jackson in collaboration with Robert Greene, this book is written for the hearts of ambitious women who wish to come up . . . and stay up!

Step-by-step, through each commandment, I will teach you how to take adversity and turn it into prosperity. Together, we will evaluate the true meaning behind the obstacles we face and utilize the strength we gain from them to come out on top! It is my desire through this book to become your morning cup of coffee and the tea you drink to calm your nerves at night. I want to keep you motivated and help you boost your self-esteem level to a 10!

It's time to take a moment to go inside and reflect. You are way stronger and more powerful than you may think!

Transformation occurs when we no longer care about what others think about us and we begin to focus on how we view ourselves. We must erase the hurt, pain, and regrets of our past, and picture in our minds becoming the ultimate image we desire to see. Before we get started, I am going to share a secret strategy I've used for many years.

Close your eyes for a second and picture the dreams you had as a little girl about your success. Take a moment and view yourself and your accomplishments just as you pictured in your dreams. This may seem stupid to some, but it really works!

Anytime fear or doubt tries to grab ahold of me, I utilize my mind to escape. The mind is our most powerful weapon. It can hurt us or help us. I envision myself to be everything I ever dreamed of in life, and I stay in that moment as long as I can. It's crazy how this simple technique fuels me. When my strength is depleted, it restores me because I have a goal, and I know I must reach it! Utilizing this simple technique, I've walked in my dream house and drove my dream car long before they became my reality. The more focused I became about my goals, the quicker they came to life!

Now it's time to transform your mind to the image of the ultimate Boss Chick who you desire to be. As you journey with me through these next several chapters, allow the words in this book to seep into your soul and reflect upon them. Following this simple step, I promise you will change your life!

What are you waiting for? It's time to turn up! Let the journey of a Boss Chick begin! It is written . . .!

CHAPTER ONE

Commandment I

"Thou Shall Love Yourself And Protect Yourself At All Cost"

REVELATION

A virtuous woman understands the importance of self-love. With this one key factor a woman can reign as a queen. Yet without it, she will be viewed as a "chickenhead." Therefore, self-love is an attribute that every Boss Chick must cultivate and guard with her whole heart!

Our self-love is the reflection of how others will view us. If a woman disrespects herself, she unconsciously gives others permission to do the same. In contrast, if a women loves, values, and honors her self-worth, she sets boundaries within the universe that commands others to follow her lead. The simple concept of self-love is powerful enough to turn even the most fragile woman into a Boss Chick. The more you love yourself, the more your inner light will radiate for others to recognize and acknowledge your true beauty. Therefore, the first step to becoming a Boss Chick is to love and protect yourself at all cost!

Many women learn how to value themselves through harsh experiences, stemming from emotional pain and rejection by men. Seeking love, attention, and affection, women often tolerate abuse. In a perfect world, it is the job of a father to teach his daughter she is a princess. Women who grow up in loving homes with the support of their dads are less likely to allow men to mistreat them, because they have been taught their self-worth. Unfortunately, women like myself, who grew up in broken homes without a father figure, are often easily manipulated by men. Our emotional insecurities caused by the absence of our fathers lead to deep-rooted abandonment issues. Therefore, we tend to stay trapped in destructive relationships because of our fear of being abandoned once again by a male figure whom we love.

There are men who prey on our insecurities. They are controlling men who feel powerless when they cannot "remote-control" their woman. Subsequently, they want to know her whereabouts at all times. This behavior may seem fine and even admirable at first, but you will quickly see the dynamics change if you happen to miss his call!

This type of man is generally verbally and physically abusive. He passionately pursues his prey, which is often misconstrued as love. The truth is, these kind of men are very insecure. Just like many women, they experienced traumatic events in their lives that have caused them to feel powerless. In an attempt to hide their own vulnerabilities, they must seek affection from women because it allows them to feel good about themselves. Instead of cherishing and respecting their queen as they should, fear of abandonment causes them to entrap her and make her his slave. This may sound sick, but it is true!

It is important to understand that neither a man nor a woman can love another being without first loving self! If a person doesn't have self-love, there is no way they can show you love, bottom line! Therefore, the first analysis a woman should take when she seeks to engage a man is to find out if he loves himself. Please analyze him thoroughly to avoid being "bamboozled." Beware, some men get into "movie mode" and pretend they're someone they're not in hopes you will find their "character" appealing. But, there will always be signs that reveal he is a fraud. If a man lives a reckless lifestyle that puts him in jeopardy, he does not love himself. If a man lacks values and integrity, he certainly does not love himself! Never ever think you can take on the task of changing a man who has no self-love. This type of individual will only resent you and try their best to make you their victim. Once again, he is incapable of truly loving anyone else, because he doesn't love himself!

Jealousy is a blatant sign of a man who lacks self-love. A jealous man will meet you as you wear a sexy outfit, yet a few months after dating, will not allow you to wear anything eye-appealing. He will spend a majority of his time seed planting in an attempt to tear down your self-image. If successful, he will make you his prey, attempting to control your every move through his mental manipulation. This type of individual is extremely insecure. In his mind, he can't understand for the life of him how such a beautiful woman entertained him, so he decides to hold on to his trophy at all costs! His manipulation begins with accusing his woman of cheating, even when he knows she has no such desire. He constantly goes through her phone and e-mails and attacks those she is associated with. It is his desire to disconnect her from anyone that can peep his "game" or those he feels inferior to. Therefore, he isolates her and feeds her so many lies until she buys into his fantasy. In the name of love, the woman then loses herself to please this man, while her life spins out of control. Her first mistake was lack of self-love.

When you truly love yourself, you are not easily influenced by the thoughts of others. Instead of being concerned with how man views you, you become more concerned with how GOD views you. A woman filled with self-love will identify a predator two blocks away. Through their initial interactions, his lack of self-love will stand out like a sore thumb. She will be repelled, saving herself unnecessary grief.

A woman filled with self-love is programmed to discern the difference between affection and love. She knows a person can be kind to you and perform a loving act without actually loving you. Therefore, the way she deciphers love from affection is by analyzing the motive behind his actions. If a man buys her a nice gift because he desires to have sex with her, she knows his gift is not a representation of his love; he simply desires to purchase a service. Subsequently, she doesn't allow material goods or baseless acts to sway her or compel her to compromise her integrity. Instead, she quickly identifies the difference between love and lust and guards her heart from predators. Her wisdom qualifies her as a Boss Chick!

A Boss Chick does not welcome a man who desires to be her "competitor." When a man illustrates he doesn't have her best interest at heart, she exits! As a result, her wisdom protects her from an envious man who will spend most of his time knocking down her self-esteem by cheating, lying, and brainwashing her, simply because of his own lack of self-love. Instead of getting stepped on, a Boss Chick steps up her game!

A Boss Chick is confident about who she is, and she loves herself, despite her flaws. A Boss Chick is a woman who never settles for less than the best for herself at all times. She constantly analyzes herself, and when she recognizes areas of her life that can utilize some improvement she takes action! A Boss Chick loves who she is because she has rolled up her sleeves and done the necessary work to become better. Instead of being envious of what other women have, a Boss Chick concentrates on what she wants and strives to get it!

A Boss Chick is not moved by the opinions of others. Instead, she becomes aligned with Almighty God, and she puts her focus on Him. A Boss Chick looks at life through both her spiritual and natural eyes. She is wise enough to recognize her beauty, and she embraces her uniqueness, no matter her circumstances. Most importantly, a Boss Chick knows it is okay to be alone, so the absence of a companion doesn't bother her. When she is lonely, she digs deep and finds fulfillment within herself.

A Boss Chick is a trendsetter. Instead of allowing others to dictate what is hot, she sets the course and others follow. A Boss Chick recognizes her strengths and addresses her weaknesses. She is wise enough to utilize her strong points to catapult her into greatness. A Boss Chick lives her life on purpose. She is focused on her goals. Constantly practicing principles of leadership, she masters her trade while others take note. Her constant success charges her self-confidence and makes her comfortable living in her own skin.

A Boss Chick acknowledges her accomplishments and openly rewards herself without regards of what others may think. Even when there are no spectators around, a Boss Chick knows how to be her own coach. Therefore, she motivates herself, and she pats herself on the back, but does not break her arms while doing so. A Boss Chick realizes at times she must stand alone. Therefore, she also knows how to become her own lover and her best friend. Instead of seeking acclamations from others, internally, she praises and admires herself. As a result, she is capable of recharging her own inner strength, which allows her to move with precision even during adversity.

Becoming a Boss Chick commands a lifestyle of self-love. This process begins with knowing who you are, being comfortable in your own skin, and discovering your purpose on earth. These attributes will protect you from allowing anyone to devalue you or compromise your self-worth. Most importantly, a Boss Chick knows she is her own greatest asset. Therefore, she protects herself at all cost!

PRACTICAL ANALYSIS

The hardships I experienced as a child caused me to develop discipline. I had intensely observed the failures of others around me, which made me determined not to make the same mistakes. Although I became successful at attaining my goals, there was always an emptiness inside I could not fix. Like most women, I desired companionship, so I looked for affection from men.

The absence of my father played a huge role in plummeting my self-esteem. As a young child, I watched TV shows like *The Cosby Show* and *Family Matters.* By watching them, I was taught that fathers were providers, protectors, problem solvers, and great listeners. I desperately wished I had the presence of my dad like the children I saw in the show. His absence made me feel less than good enough. Searching to fill the void of not having a male figure in my life left me vulnerable and dissatisfied.

Once I reached the age of dating and became intimate with a man, this experience rocked my world! I wasn't prepared for the emotional roller-coaster ride I encountered. Blinded by what appeared to be ultimate happiness, I finally thought I had what I was missing, and I was determined to hold on to it by any means necessary! Consequently, I opened the door to a cycle of damaged relationships with men that diminished my self-esteem even more.

Before writing this chapter, I had to pray heavily and ask God Almighty for strength to get through this without opening old wounds. I want to make it clear I don't claim to be perfect; I am still a work in progress. After many years of putting in the work to fix my flaws and deal with my past experiences, I am still in the healing process. The only difference is now I am empowered to recognize the truth and take action when needed. Today, I've learned to put myself first, which keeps me protected.

I was honestly going to focus on one relationship in particular that shadowed some of the darkest moments in my life, but there is no way you could learn from me if I only shared one story. Therefore, I am going to share multiple stories with you as practical references for this chapter. Collectively, these destructive relationships helped me learn if I didn't value myself, I wouldn't be valued by others. Through many sleepless nights, several heartbreaks, continuous depression, embarrassment, isolation, breakdowns and loss of ambition, I realized I had to seek refuge from God instead of men. By sharing my costly mistakes, it is my hope you will avoid my mishaps and/or break loose from destructive relationships that may be holding you bound.

Being ambitious and having an outgoing personality caused me to attract different types of men. At first, their intentions may have been strictly to seek sexual gratification, but after getting to know me, they always seemed to want much more. I believe I intrigued them by my intellect and my drive, which they seemed to admire. Attending school, having a job, no children, and being capable of holding a conversation with an extensive vocabulary made me a standout for a "hood chick." Additionally, my street smarts appealed to a lot of hustlers, scammers, and quick talkers, who, I assumed, felt it was an asset to have a "ride-or-die" chick on their team. As a result, it was never hard to find male companionship.

I always believed in honesty, so I opened up and shared my life with my partners. I thought if I shared the truth about my experiences and the fact I had an absent father, it would allow them to understand my pain, and they would help me to heal. I was wrong! The secrets I shared only gave these individuals ammunition to hurt me even more. From this experience, I learned weak men seek out "wounded" women because it is easier to manipulate them.

Each failed relationship exposed more of my flaws which I began to despise. I realized behind my confident smile was a fragile woman who feared being alone. It wasn't financial gratification that attracted me to men; it was more of an emotional need to fill my inner void. I wanted to be validated, loved, and appreciated, and I thought only a man could satisfy my needs. Therefore, I passionately sought after "Mr. Right."

When I first started dating, I believed if I was educated, drove a nice car, had a good job, and knew how to cook and clean, I would attract the man I desired. If he saw I was the "complete package," my task would be easy . . . or so I thought. This man would love me, cherish me, and never cheat on me, just like the storybooks. I figured I would find my king and live in a nice house in the suburbs, behind a white picket fence. In my head, I had all the details figured out, but I lacked one solid truth about being a queen. It's not a king who makes a queen. A queen is groomed and polished for many years before she is chosen by a king. She honors and loves herself, which radiates her inner beauty. As a result, she attracts the likeness of her image, drawing her to her king. Too bad I didn't understand this principle long ago. I would have saved myself many heartaches!

I met my first love at 18 years old, while working at Mc Donald's to help pay for my college tuition. I was focused. And, I have to admit, I was sort of cute in my tightly fitted khaki pants that filled my full-figure frame, which I wore along with my "Mickey D's" visor cocked to the side. I was immediately scouted out as he made his way to my register to spit his game. I wasn't interested at first, but his hot pursuit of me intrigued me. I took note he was just as ambitious as I was, which attracted me to him. He was several years older than I, and he had money, intellect, and a very nice ride. His conversation kept me intrigued as he schooled me on things I never dreamed about. After a short period of time, not only did he take hold of my mind, he also captured my heart. Not understanding the power of love or wrong intentions, I quickly became an addict. I wanted the rush I felt in the inner beauty of my soul for this man to last forever. Consequently, I was willing to give my all to be with him, and I did!

I moved out of my mother's house and moved in with him. When my Prince Charming realized he had me just where he wanted me, he became more like a jailor than a companion. He began to track my every move and worked hard to kill what was left of my self-esteem. He told me vicious lies about my self-worth, and like a fool, I believed him. In a matter of months, I had quit my job, dropped out of college, and turned into his housewife. Not too long after, I also became his punching bag. He used me, and abused me, until I completely lost myself. I knew I was in a dark place where I shouldn't have been, but my desire to be loved caused me to stay. For almost 2 years I stayed stuck, accepting his abuse that also included infidelity. After what I perceived to be endless pain, coupled with suicidal thoughts, the power of prayer broke me free from my jailor. After I finally got the strength to let go, my life seemed to come back together just as quickly as I lost it. I reenrolled back in school, landed a job at a Fortune 500 company, and was ready to move forward and take on the world!

Mistake #1—Instead of allowing myself to heal from the destructive relationship I just came out of, I used another man, who I will call “Mr. Rebound,” to help me get over my pain. This began my destructive cycle of poisonous relationships. Each relationship that followed lasted from 2 to 7 years, making it very difficult to just move on. One after another, I used each man to get over another. In my mind, I was getting ahead, yet with each destructive relationship I encountered, I lost more of myself.

Despite my hardships, I never lost my ambition. Remember, I felt in order to be a good catch I had to have my professional and home life in order. Looking back, I don’t know if that actually helped or hindered me. I had a partner at one point who was a felon that worked odd jobs. I still loved him despite his decisions in life, but I felt I owed him loyalty because he helped me get over the pain of my last relationship.

After getting to know him a little better, I began to realize he was a wounded man with insecurity issues. He wasn’t very handsome, which may have caused him to despise the attention I received from others. I can remember at the age of 20 I purchased a new 5 Series BMW. He told me this car would gain me the wrong attention, so he tried to sway me from purchasing it. I didn’t take his advice, which caused major havoc! Shortly after I got the car, his behavior changed drastically; he became extremely controlling. Overnight, he started abusing me both mentally and physically. I gave him plenty of ultimatums to seek help, but he showed me by way of action that he could care less about my demands. I cried, not understanding why our relationship took such a major turn, and I blamed the purchase of my car. Truth is, it was deeper than that!

"Mr. Rebound" was what I call a jealous competitor. Secretly, he was competing with me. After opening up several pieces of mail which included auto loan denials, I learned he actually wanted what I had. This man didn't want me to receive more shine than he, so his goal was to block my success. Beating myself up for allowing the car to come between us blinded me from seeing the truth; he was insecure!

I had another relationship for several years with a man who I will refer to as "Mr. Womanizer." This dude had to have all the attention, at all times. If I didn't give him the attention he so desired, he would get it from whoever would entertain him. His friendly flirting quickly turned into aggressive cheating. When I caught him engaging in infidelities, he often made excuses and shifted the blame on me. His absurd reasoning was I did not have sex with him enough. He failed to take into consideration that his ongoing cheating made me reluctant to be intimate with him. It also caused us to lose our connection, yet I stayed around, hoping things would eventually change. After confronting several of the women he "jumped off" with, I thought something was wrong with me. He often cheated on me with young girls who had little education, zero responsibilities, and lived with their parents. His cheating caused me to feel inadequate. It wasn't until much later that I realized he chose younger girls because they wanted to have fun, and they were easier to impress. They were actually pawns he used to boost his ego and cover up his low self-esteem. At the time, I had no clue that I had no power to fix what was missing inside of himself—self-love. Without the strength to break away, I decided to get even. Trapped in this dysfunctional relationship, I became a cheater. I wanted "Mr. Womanizer" to feel the same pain I felt, but instead, I only caused myself more heartache. I wasn't built out of the same cloth as he. My conscious wouldn't allow me to turn into the monster that he helped create. Staring at an image I no longer recognized in the mirror, once again, I prayed for the strength to let go, but it wasn't easy!

Looking back, it was like I was under a spell. I wanted to be loved so badly, I was willing to compromise myself. I didn't understand my value in the relationship, and I had no idea of my self-worth. This is no longer the case today!

Experience has taught me that two-halves in a relationship can never make a whole. You get from the table what you put in. If you don't love yourself and set boundaries, no man will ever respect you or treat you right. A broken individual who doesn't love him or herself cannot love anyone else.

Furthermore, a man doesn't have the power to heal another individual. God is our healer. Therefore, spiritual matters must be handled by Him. If your life is spinning out of control and you find yourself caring for someone else more than you love yourself, break free and seek refuge in God.

You cannot be a Boss Chick if you do not value your greatest asset, which is yourself. Therefore, value yourself, love yourself, and protect yourself at all cost!

JEWEL DROPS

- With self-love a woman can reign as a queen. Without it, she'll be viewed as a "chickenhead."
- Our self-love is the reflection of how others will view us. If a woman disrespects herself, she unconsciously gives others permission to do the same.
- Neither a man nor a woman can love another being without first loving self! Therefore, if a person doesn't love himself or herself, never think he or she will love you; they can't!
- Jealousy is a blatant sign of a man who lacks self-love. Never engage a man who wishes to be your competitor or you will hurt yourself in the process.
- When you truly love yourself, you are not easily influenced by the thoughts of others. Instead of being concerned with how man views you, you become more concerned with how GOD views you.
- A woman filled with self-love doesn't allow material goods or baseless acts to sway her or compel her to compromise her integrity. Instead, she quickly identifies the differ-

ence between love and lust and guards her heart from predators, at all costs!

- A Boss Chick is confident about who she is and she loves herself, despite her flaws. When she recognizes areas of her life that can utilize improvement, she takes action! She loves who she is because she has rolled up her sleeves and done the necessary work to become better.
- A Boss Chick looks at life through both her spiritual and natural eyes. She is wise enough to recognize her beauty, and she embraces her uniqueness. No matter her circumstances, she is able to reign victoriously, because with this gift she is able to discern the truth!
- A Boss Chick knows it is okay to be alone, so the absence of a companion doesn't bother her. When she is lonely she digs deep and finds fulfillment within herself.
- A Boss Chick knows how to be her own coach, even when there are no spectators around. Therefore, she holds the key to her own motivation and is capable of recharging her inner strength at any time. This allows her to move with precision, even during adversity!

CHAPTER TWO

Commandment II

"Thou Shall 'Boss Up' or Get 'Bossed Around'"

REVELATION

The key characteristic that distinguishes a Boss Chick from others is her courage. She is a woman that has done the necessary work to overcome her fears, so she faces all opponents and obstacles head-on. Instead of running away from opportunities because of fear of failure, a Boss Chick gladly embraces challenges. She works hard, sets goals, and plans to win, even when others have counted her out!

In the face of adversity, a Boss Chick doesn't panic, and she refuses to quit! Her understanding about the purpose of obstacles keeps her rooted and grounded, because she realizes even her failures will eventually catapult her to success. During stormy seasons, a Boss Chick knows how to pace herself. When she gets tired, she takes a moment to rest and allows herself to regroup. Instead of relying solely on her own strength, a Boss Chick relies on power and direction from Almighty God. Therefore, she is never disappointed, and she always stays ahead!

A Boss Chick is never too proud to seek the assistance of others. When she faces challenges, she seeks out wisdom from other successful individuals. A Boss Chick stays on top of her game! She constantly researches and reads books to stimulate her mind and empower her to achieve her goals. She understands in a changing world she must be capable of reinventing herself. Therefore, she scouts out new innovative developments and gains insight in her area of expertise, which positions her to stay on top!

A Boss Chick is a woman who stands her ground. Her "yes" means "yes," and her "no" means "absolutely not!" She is strong and methodical in her thinking and takes into consideration the consequences before she proceeds to act. Therefore, she remains protected, while also protecting the interest of others, and she is successful!

A Boss Chick is a woman who has mastered the art of being a boss. A true boss is a leader who commands respect from her peers. She is the driving force that keeps everything together! A Boss Chick is very influential. She helps organize and manage the work of others, ultimately benefiting not only herself but her entire team!

A Boss Chick understands the power of strategy. Therefore, she works smarter, not harder. She utilizes her talents to attract others with similar interests, and inspires them to achieve their goals. A Boss Chick lives by the rule: there is no "i" in "team." Therefore, she is a true team player. If her teammates should ever fall short or run into obstacles, she is there to troubleshoot, take action, and champions them to the finish line!

A Boss Chick's light radiates for the world to see. Her inner confidence won't allow her to compromise her morals or integrity because she has way too much to lose. A Boss Chick is not a people pleaser. Instead, she aims to please God. She remains grounded, and her accomplishments inspire others to follow her lead.

A Boss Chick knows her self-worth, and she knows her purpose on earth. Therefore, she aligns her goals accordingly and remains focused on the prize. A Boss Chick understands she is never alone. She has the help of the Almighty God and the host of angels to help fulfill her purpose. Subsequently, a Boss Chick is not prideful or cocky. Instead, she acknowledges God uses her as a vessel, part of His bigger plan. Her combination of power and humility shines boldly, causing others to flock to her and follow her lead.

Being a Boss Chick comes with responsibility. At times sacrifices have to be made in order to achieve her goals.

Therefore, she is always ready to work hard to accomplish what may seem impossible to others. A Boss Chick is never scared of failure, because she understands that every challenge, including failures, gives her an opportunity to learn more and to become stronger. Therefore, a Boss Chick makes plans, and she acts on them! She is disciplined and doesn't allow distractions get in the way of success. Instead, she moves with precision and executes all her goals!

Becoming a Boss Chick takes time and experience. One must first come to the realization she must "boss up" or get "bossed around"! Grasping this principle will give you the fuel to change your life!

PRACTICAL ANALYSIS

Growing up, I worked super hard to escape poverty. Some of my girlfriends tried their hand at dating dudes for "come ups," in hopes "his" money would modify "her" lifestyle, but that wasn't conducive for me. I observed their needy behavior along with the disrespectful treatment that followed. This destructive combination led to a constant cycle of failed relationships, caused by their gold-digging addiction. Observing the chaos in their lives made me realize this wasn't the road I wanted to follow. They were "treadmilling" or "running but getting nowhere fast." With the realization that I would have to create my own path, I decided to use education as my weapon to overcome poverty. Therefore, I jumped in full force earning my associate's in legal studies from New York Paralegal School, followed by my bachelor of science in criminal justice from John Jay College in New York.

After I procured my degrees I felt I had the tools needed to win. I landed a legal manager position at a prestigious law firm in Garden City, New York, where I was content. My leadership skills made me a shining star! My bosses were attorneys who relied on me to research and prepare legal documents. One day, one of my bosses had a family emergency, leaving me to handle this one particular client who required specialized service. When my efforts were successful, a revelation struck me like a bolt of lightning. I finally understood I was capable of performing on my own, without my boss. This experience made me realize that my true success would not occur until I "bossed up." For way too long, I had allowed the comfort of my job security to distract me from the desire to be extraordinary. This is a dilemma many women face. Therefore, my advice to every Boss Chick is to never get so comfortable you allow your present status to hinder the plans you desire to achieve. Always aspire to want more experience, salary, and security, then work hard to gain it!

When I suffered hardships in my personal life that led to difficulties at my job, I received a pink slip. Yes, girl, I got fired! After several years of loyalty and dedication to this firm, the partners I slaved for had no problem letting me go! After being smacked in the face, suddenly I had an epiphany. They never appreciated me as an asset, so for years I was merely on "borrowed time." This ordeal was devastating!

While receiving a measly $405 a week from unemployment, I researched high-demand services needed in the New York area. Real estate was at one of its highest peaks in 2006. I went back to school and obtained licenses in real estate, appraisal, and notary services. I also received New York certifications for property management and title closing. Desperate to achieve success, I mustered up the faith to utilize my savings and limited resources to start my own firm. Practicing as a paralegal and a real estate consultant, I opened "Sunny Legal Realty Group." In 1 year I acquired more revenue in my new occupation as a boss than I made at my last job as an employee.

My success gave me faith and newfound hope. I realized through this obstacle, I was stronger and more powerful than I ever imagined! My first step in achieving success was "bossing up." If I had never tried my hand as an entrepreneur I would probably be stagnant and unstable today. Everything happens for a reason is a true statement that relates to my experience. This bump in the road that hindered me was actually a blessing in disguise!

I could have sat back in my success and not challenged myself further, but I didn't. Starting my own business gave me the ability to recognize I was good at sales. Shortly after setting up Sunny Legal Realty Group, I was given the opportunity to be a partner and help open an upscale shoe boutique. At the time, I knew little about the shoe business, but I had a love for trendy shoes. I researched the market and discovered it was an opportunity I'd like to explore.

In June 2011, I became co-owner of Je T'aime Shoes, located in Brooklyn, New York. We opened our location 1 year prior to Barclay Center Stadium opening. Once again, I rolled up my sleeves and did tons of research to attract new customers. With the new wave of social media and celebrity clients my partner and I attracted, we were able to take the shoe market by storm! To date, our store has been on several reality shows. We are constantly strategizing and creating new ideas to increase sales. It's a combination of our hard work, dedication, research, and customer service that has kept our business in the lead. In the next 5 years, God willing, I see Je T'aime Shoes expanding to several cities throughout the U.S. This would never have been possible if I didn't overcome my fear of venturing out of my 9–5 job to explore the world of business. I had to learn by experience the power of "bossing up!"

The main obstacle that stands in the way of many women is the fear of failure. We don't want to be laughed at or told . . . "I knew you could never do that." We remain trapped in mediocrity, when we are actually destined for greatness. Therefore, we must not let "haters" or fear take us off the divine course God has destined for our lives.

Are you stuck in a state you don't wish to be in? Is something inside of you telling you that you should aspire for more? Utilize my experience as inspiration and spread your wings and fly! You have more to gain than you do to lose, so what are you waiting for?

Boss ladies, it's time to take hold of your future and capture your dreams! "Boss Up!"

JEWEL DROPS

- Courage is the key factor that distinguishes a Boss Chick from others. She is a woman who has pulled up her sleeves and done the work to overcome her fears.
- In the face of adversity a Boss Chick doesn't panic—nor does she quit! Her understanding about the purpose of obstacles keeps her rooted and grounded because she realizes even her failures will catapult her to success.
- A Boss Chick never relies solely on her own strength. Instead, she seeks power and direction from Almighty God. Therefore, she is never disappointed, and she always stays ahead.
- A Boss Chick constantly researches and reads books that stimulate her mind and empower her to achieve her goals. Therefore, reading is an essential part of her success.
- A Boss Chick understands in a changing world she must be capable of reinventing herself. Therefore, she scouts out new innovative developments and insights in her area of expertise, which positions her to stay on top!
- A Boss Chick is a woman who stands her ground. Her "yes" means "yes," and her "no" means "absolutely not!" She is strong and methodical in her thinking. Therefore, she always remains protected.

- A Boss Chick comprehends the power of strategy. Therefore, she works smarter, not harder. She utilizes her talents to attract others with similar interest, and inspires them to achieve their goals.
- A Boss Chick lives by one rule! There is no "i" in "team." Therefore, she is a true team player. If her teammates should ever fall short or run into obstacles, she is there to troubleshoot, take action, and champion them to the finish line!
- A Boss Chick understands she is never alone. She has the help of the Almighty God and the host of angels to help execute her purpose. Therefore, she is not prideful or cocky, yet she acknowledges God uses her as a vessel, part of His bigger plan.
- A Boss Chick is never scared of failure because she understands that with every challenge, including failures, it gives her an opportunity to learn more and to become stronger. Therefore, she makes plans and acts on them, without fear!

CHAPTER THREE

Commandment III

"Thou Shall Be A Goal-Digger, Not A Gold-Digger"

REVELATION

A Boss Chick is an independent woman who functions well with or without the companionship of another. She is an educated woman who masters self-love and works hard to reach her greatest potential. A Boss Chick capitalizes on her strengths, while addressing her weaknesses. She has goals and great aspirations for her life, which are dependent upon her own skills and talents. Therefore, she is not enamored by the riches of others, because she is equipped to go out and get her own!

A Boss Chick understands the power of her beauty, yet she does not overly depend upon this attribute to sustain her well-being. Instead, her wisdom protects her from entering relationships solely to seek financial gain. She realizes giving up her independence will ultimately cause her to lose control over her life.

A Boss Chick is a woman who desires to be equally yoked with her partner. Although he is a good provider, who admires and respects her, she still brings her own contributions to the table. She is considered to be an asset to any relationship, not a liability. Even if she finds a wealthy, compatible partner, she stays true to her purpose and continues to build her own empire. As a result, whether she is with a mate or not, she still reigns as queen in her own right. It's her self-love and wisdom that certifies her as a Boss Chick!

A Boss Chick works intensely on self-improvement. As a result, she loves the reflection she sees in the mirror. Her focus is not seeking a better "him," but how to become a better "her." She is not worried about your money, his money, nor their money. Instead, a Boss Chick is concerned about her money. Therefore, she doesn't idolize or envy the accomplishments of others, nor does she seek after the things they have. Her wisdom guides her to focus on her own skill sets and talents, driving her to research what is needed to procure her own riches.

A Boss Chick stays in her financial lane. She takes pride in her profession and values the revenue she receives from her hard work. Even though she has great aspirations for her life, she knows there will always be others who have more material riches. Therefore, a Boss Chick does not covet her neighbor's riches. Instead, she utilizes the success of others as a reminder she too can accomplish her dreams.

A Boss Chick understands the detriment of trying to keep up with the "Joneses." Therefore, she never engages in competition with others, especially when she knows the "Joneses" don't reside on her block. She is a woman of integrity who lives within her means. She does not buy material possessions simply to impress others; she stays in her financial lane and rewards herself in measures she can afford. Therefore, she remains successful!

A Boss Chick knows the power she has is based on her independence and leadership skills. Subsequently, she is never willing to compromise these attributes, no matter what she stands to gain. She is a bona fide "get-money" chick who doesn't mind putting in the hard work. She guards her reputation wholeheartedly, only allowing her best quality work to be associated with her name. Although a Boss Chick works hard, she is skillfully calculated in her execution. She understands the concept, if she's given a fish she can eat today, but if she is taught how to fish, she can eat for a lifetime. Therefore, she seeks mentors over handouts, which ultimately increases her wealth.

A Boss Chick is a woman with insight. She is constantly planning and setting goals. Before she leaves her home each day she generates a "To-Do" list. She realizes a lot of women "don't plan to fail," we merely "fail to plan." Therefore, by establishing structure she stays on track and achieves her goals, because she leaves no room for distractions. She is full of self-esteem and confidence, because she knows who she is, and where she is going. A Boss Chick is protected by her purpose, which positions her for greatness. She knows the only barrier between her dreams and reality is her faith and imagination. Therefore, she dreams big and uses her tenacity, hard work, and dedication to make her dreams come true.

A Boss Chick constantly looks for ways to sharpen her skills. She spends time reading and researching ventures that may be profitable. A Boss Chick knows all great things require work. Therefore, she is willing to dedicate substantial time to work on self-improvement. She is a woman who values wisdom and knowledge. Seeking out inspiration, she surrounds herself with like-minded individuals, and she forms a circle of friends from whom she can learn. By doing so, she stays motivated and becomes an ultimate Goal-Digger! Guarded by these principles, she reigns as a true Boss Chick who stays on top of her game!

PRACTICAL ANALYSIS

We live in a society where women are taught to seek men who are wealthy to secure their futures. As a result, many women enter relationships for all the wrong reasons. Instead of looking for love and compatibility, which is the glue for long-term relationships, these women simply scout out riches. Women of this nature are generally described as "gold-diggers" or "groupies." They are so enamored with the accomplishments and wealth of another individual, they are willing to make this person their god. Instead of trusting in the Almighty God to be their provider, they mistakenly put all their trust in man. All seems well at first, when they conquer their mission to obtain wealth. But, this type of relationship ALWAYS has a disastrous ending! When the storms of life come (and they will come!) and the weak foundation of their relationship washes away, these women are left with nothing! Their wrong motives catch up to them, and Karma kicks in. Consequently, the very thing they sought so passionately is taken away, and they are left to start over at square one. Instead of spending their time working to improve themselves, they utilize their time to chase someone else's riches. As a result, when the relationship dissolves, they have no way of maintaining the same luxurious lifestyle on their own, making their lives miserable and often unbearable. All who seek after the riches or esteem of others and neglect working on themselves will experience this very same fate. I've watched this story repeatedly, and it makes my stomach churn!

In this chapter, I will share several practical examples with you to enlighten you to the detriment of being a "gold-digger" and the virtue of being a "goal-digger."

Ladies, take off your stilettos, grab a pen and pad, then get comfy. Class is now in session!

EXAMPLE ONE ———

Shaunice was a pretty girl who lived in the Amsterdam Housing Projects in Manhattan, New York. Shaunice's mom was a drug addict who had several children, of which Shaunice was the eldest. While her mother was out getting high, Shaunice was left to care for her younger siblings. Oftentimes, she missed school when her mother took off on long binges, which caused her to eventually drop out.

With little money to care for her siblings, Shaunice had few options. Walking to the corner store one day, she caught the attention of a local drug dealer, Rahiem aka Rah. Shaunice's caramel skin, long hair, and curvaceous body immediately caught his attention; Rah's flashy lifestyle, wealth, and car attracted hers. Rah, who was 20 years old at the time, and Shaunice, who had just turned 16, hooked up and instantly hit it off! Shaunice saw Rah as a means to escape poverty. Therefore, she put her best game on and proceeded to collect on her big payday!

Life quickly changed for Shaunice. Rah bought her a nice house in New Jersey and gave her the ability to move her family to this new dwelling, making her the happiest girl on earth. She finally felt she was in position to live happily ever after, courtesy of her provider, Rah, the drug kingpin.

* * *

Tamika grew up in Mount Vernon, New York, in a nice middle-class area. Her mother was a school principal, and her father owned a successful construction company. Tamika was well provided for under one condition: she had to attend school and maintain an "A" average.

Tamika was perceived as weird in her neighborhood, because she made her school studies her focus. She maintained straight A's, was always on the honor roll, and received several academic awards. The children she looked up to often made fun of her and called her a "nerd," secretly envying her accomplishments. Tamika was an attractive young lady, but the constant bullying caused her to withdraw and develop low-self-esteem.

One day, Carolyn, who was considered a popular girl in the high school, decided to befriend Tamika. Carolyn was failing biology and needed Tamika to tutor her. Tamika tutored her and through their interactions Carolyn began to actually like Tamika. To show her gratitude, Carolyn decided to give Tamika a makeover and introduce her to some of her guy friends. Tamika was so excited to have a "cool" friend like Carolyn she was willing to do anything in her power to please her.

Carolyn took Tamika to a party at the Roxy Roller Skating Rink in New York City where she met Rah. He drove a brand-new Mercedes-Benz that captivated the attention of all the girls at the party. His Rolex watch flooded in diamonds were in sync with the diamond Cuban link chain that blinded the eyes of the girls who were enamored by him, which included Carolyn and her friends. Despite the advances from many of the girls at the party who sought his attention, his focus was on Tamika. Carolyn urged Tamika to talk to Rah, and they hooked up. Shortly thereafter, Rah made Tamika his girl, but she had no idea about Shaunice, Rah's main girlfriend who resided with him in New Jersey.

After meeting Rah, Tamika lost her focus. Driving her man's luxury cars caught the eyes of those who once teased her in her neighborhood. Overnight she became a "cool" kid; she was determined to guard her new reputation at all costs! Consequently, her grades plummeted, and her only focus was maintaining her popularity. She was hooked by the fame and attention Rah's lifestyle brought her.

Rah was attracted to Tamika's wisdom and her family background. Just like Shaunice, he was born and raised in the projects, so he liked the fact he had what he called a "house-chick." Nevertheless, he was still not going to get rid of his main chick, Shaunice, so he decided to have them both. Eventually, they both found out about each other, but neither woman was willing to let him go. They both saw him as a great provider despite his cheating, so they were willing to accept his infidelities that included more than just the two of them. Taking turns sharing Rah's affection became normal over time. Eventually the back and forth was tiring to Rah, so he urged the women to engage in threesomes to further gain his love. Hooked in and totally dependent upon Rah's finances, the girls simply took orders and catered to their man. Although they felt in control because they had access to his money, they actually were pawns in his chess game of life.

Several years went by and both girls stayed faithful to Rah. Tamika even abandoned her family who disapproved of her lifestyle. Well provided for, sporting luxury cars, and living in fine homes with substantial money in the bank, neither of the women seemed to have a care in the world. All was well—until the FEDS raided Tamika's house and found 14 kilos of crack cocaine.

Refusing to cooperate against Rah, Tamika, who was only 22 years old, was given a hefty 27-year federal sentence. With little evidence against him, Rah was able to negotiate a plea deal for a 10-year mandatory minimum sentence, but had to walk away with no assets, forfeiting the homes, luxury cars, and his money to the government.

Flat broke with no stash money or education, Shaunice and her family were forced to stay with relatives in a Queens, New York, public housing project. Realizing this arrangement wouldn't last long, Shaunice had to make quick money to make ends meet. Therefore, she became an exotic dancer at a nightclub in the Bronx. While stripping, Shaunice met another drug dealer who was attracted by her beauty. She immediately latched on, believing he would help her regain the lifestyle she once enjoyed. Just like Rah, he bought her a nice house, took care of her family, and convinced her to quit stripping.

Life seemed like it was coming back together for Shaunice . . . until she found out she was in her first trimester of pregnancy. After extensive testing, the doctor told her she was diagnosed with HIV. Hysterical and shaken up, she went to inform her boyfriend of the results. He immediately got tested, but his results came back negative. Shaunice realized her current man, who was her unborn baby's father, was not the culprit. Devastated and in pursuit of answers, Shaunice decided to visit Rah, who she hadn't spoken to in years. He was housed at Fort Dix Federal Correctional Institution in New Jersey at that time.

As she waited for him to come out in his prison suit, her heart raced. She sat patiently in the waiting room taking notice of a frail man who sat beside her.

"Is your name Shaunice?" the man asked as she made eye contact with him.

"Yeah, why? Do I know you?" Shaunice questioned.

"No, but I know you! Why the hell are you coming to see my man now, you gold-digging bitch?" the man said angrily in a flamboyant tone as he snapped his fingers in her face. Shaunice stood in disbelief, shocked at the thought of Rah actually dating men. Tears flooded her eyes as she realized the intense consequences of her lifestyle. Shortly after, Rah came in the visiting room and kissed his gay lover in front of Shaunice, confirming her suspicion.

"For real, Rah? You get down like that? I guess you both should know I have HIV," Shaunice angrily blurted out, hoping to cut them deeply.

"Oh that's nothing new! Rah and I have had the virus for years. How do you think you got it?" Rah's lover said proudly.

"What?" Shaunice questioned in disbelief.

"Yeah, you played me and left me in here for dead, and now you got played! That's what you get for being a gold-digger," Rah said as he laughed and terminated her visit.

Both Shaunice and Tamika's life was ruined by Rah. Shaunice chased after the almighty dollar, and Tamika chased after fame and acceptance. In the end, the results for both of the women were the same. They both suffered mishaps and misfortunes as a result of their gold-digging behavior . . . Who's next?

EXAMPLE TWO ———

Lisa and Pamela were roommates where they attended Howard University back in the '90s. Lisa was an ambitious Chicago native who majored in journalism. Pamela was a pretty cheerleader from New York City who majored in political science and had aspirations of being a prestigious U.S. politician. Both girls worked hard to pursue their goals, with hopes they would obtain a better lifestyle for themselves.

As captain of the cheerleading squad, Pamela was extremely popular. Her beauty and intellect attracted John, the top player on the basketball team. At first glance, Pamela was not interested in dating John, as he wasn't very eye-appealing. Knowing he was the star of the basketball team, however, she allowed John to take her out on a few dates, only to find out his conversation was boring. As a result, she never entertained him again.

During her sophomore year, Pamela experienced an extreme amount of stress keeping up with her studies. She started looking for an easy way out, as she feared not being able to successfully complete school. Just as she felt like giving up, she found out John was drafted to the NBA. He was given an enormous contract, making him one of the highest-paid rookies in the league.

Immediately, Pamela called John to congratulate him and asked if he wanted to go out for dinner to celebrate. John accepted her offer, and the two of them began dating. Almost instantly, John fell in love with Pamela and asked her to relocate to his new residence in Miami. Pamela accepted his offer, quit college, and moved to Miami where John would be playing for the Miami Heat.

Following behind John, Pamela abandoned her goals and dreams in order to gain his esteem. After successfully winning him over, Pamela became his very wealthy wife. They resided in a huge mansion on Star Island. Pamela was able to live the life of her dreams, without any hard work or a care in the world. With nothing but free time on her hands, she became addicted to shopping. Each month she would spend more time spending money than actually being a wife. John never minded her spending, because he finally had the trophy bride he so desperately desired on his arm. His money afforded him the woman he couldn't obtain on his own, so he was pleased. Blinded by her beauty he failed to take notice of Pamela's male friends who she constantly kept switching. Pamela was never sexually pleased by John, so she often cheated to feed her sexual appetite.

One day while playing ball, John tore his ACL, which ultimately ended his basketball career. His contract ended, and he no longer had money flowing in. In an effort to save the rest of his fortune, he began to order his wife to cut back on her elaborate spending habits. This caused their relationship tremendous stress. The couple experienced numerous difficulties, yet with no way to support herself Pamela stayed. In fear of losing Pamela, John still allowed her to squander money on frivolous things. Eventually the couple went bankrupt. With nowhere to go after the foreclosure of their home, Pamela left John and decided to temporarily stay with her old college roommate, Lisa, who became an award-winning journalist.

Pamela entered Lisa's home and was enamored by her high-end lifestyle her stellar career afforded her. With hopes of gaining the esteem of her old college roommate, Pamela attempted to become Lisa's new lover. Although Lisa was proudly a lesbian, she recognized Pamela's motives and quickly rejected her advances.

Today, Pamela resides on a large farm in Texas, far away from the fast-paced life she was accustomed to, where she is utterly miserable. Her new spouse Bob, who is 40 years older than she, is a wealthy oil-tycoon who is not expecting to live too much longer. Her hope is she will inherit his riches and finally live the life of her dreams. Until then, her chase still continues . . .

SUMMATION

The life of a gold-digger is like a crap shoot. Some seem to get lucky at first, but eventually they ALL lose their zeal. You cannot be happy or truly successful on earth without fulfilling your purpose, which is the assignment God specifically created you to accomplish. There are certain desires that have been programmed in each of our hearts, which are connected to our purpose. These desires may decrease at times, yet they never go away. If we freeload and ride on someone else's dreams, while neglecting our own aspirations, we will create an insatiable inner void no man or material possession can fix. This inner void creates internal chaos and depression, which leads us on a chase to find fulfillment. Some seek alcohol or drugs to soothe their emptiness; others utilize people, places, or things to find relief. Despite the temporary satisfaction they may gain, this inner void remains. It can only be fixed by following God's plan for their lives, and fulfilling their purpose. Many don't understand this powerful principle, but now you do!

Ladies, it's important to know that a "freeloader's" welcome pass will eventually expire. Gold diggers are disposable liabilities, with ulterior motives. A man will never value a woman who simply seeks to drink his wine, yet doesn't partake in the picking of the grapes. You are God's wonderful creation who was built to achieve greatness. Therefore, spend the necessary time to work on yourself, develop your strengths, and find your purpose.

If you want to be happy and live a prosperous life that no other being can control, choose to be a goal-digger and you will remain on top!

JEWEL DROPS

- A Boss Chick is an independent woman who functions well without the companionship of another. She is an educated woman who masters self-love and works hard to reach her greatest potential.

  A Boss Chick has goals and great aspirations for her life, which are dependent upon her own skills and talents. Therefore, she is not enamored by the riches of others, because she is equipped to go out and get her own!
- A Boss Chick understands the power of her beauty, yet she does not overly depend upon this attribute to sustain her well-being. Instead, her wisdom protects her from entering relationships solely to seek financial gain, because she realizes by giving up her independence she will ultimately lose control over her life.
- A Boss Chick is looked upon as an asset to any relationship, not a liability. Even if she finds a wealthy, compatible partner, she stays true to her purpose and continues to build her own empire. As a result, whether she is with a mate or not, she still reigns as queen in her own right.
- A Boss Chick works intensely on self-improvement. As a result, she loves the reflection she sees in the mirror. Therefore, she doesn't idolize or envy the accomplish-

ments of others, nor does she seek after the things they have. Instead, she seeks to procure her own riches.

- A Boss Chick understands the detriment of trying to keep up with the "Joneses." Therefore, she never engages in competition with others, specifically when she knows the "Joneses" don't reside on her block. Instead, she stays in her financial lane and rewards herself in measures she can afford.
- A Boss Chick understands the concept, if she's given a fish she can eat today, but if she is taught how to fish she can eat for life. Therefore, she seeks out mentors over handouts, which ultimately increases her wealth.

A Boss Chick is a woman with insight. She is constantly planning and setting goals. She realizes a lot of women "don't plan to fail," we merely "fail to plan." Therefore, by establishing structure she stays on track and achieves her goals, because she leaves no room for distractions.

- There are certain desires that have been programmed in each of our hearts, which are connected to our purpose, that may decrease at times, yet never go away. If we freeload and ride on someone else's dreams, while neglecting our own aspirations, we will create an insatiable inner void no man can fix. Therefore, a Boss Chick lives life on purpose!
- A "freeloader's" welcome pass will eventually expire. A man will never value a woman who simply seeks to drink the wine, yet doesn't partake in picking the grapes to make it. Therefore, make sure you are an asset in your relationships, and make your true contribution!

CHAPTER FOUR

Commandment IV

"Thou Shall Be Better, Not Bitter!"

REVELATION

Life is similar to an obstacle course. There are certain challenges we must face, which will educate us, strengthen us, and ultimately help us grow. There is no such thing as avoiding life's hardships. Without obstacles we would all remain stagnant and unequipped to move to the next level. Therefore, hardships serve as essential elements for success!

A Boss Chick is a woman who understands the true purpose of life's obstacles and uses them as motivation to move ahead. Instead of allowing adversity to make her bitter, she uses it as the driving force to make her better! Her wisdom equips her to reign as queen.

Oftentimes in life, we veer off the course God has destined for us. Caught up in the chase to obtain self-fulfillment, we embark on baseless journeys that consume our attention. Therefore, God allows certain obstacles to appear, which cause us to take note, change our path, and propel us into His planned purpose for our lives. Instead of attempting to avoid challenges that arise, a Boss Chick faces them head-on and takes the time to discover the opportunities that lie within them. Her wisdom positions her to rejoice when others run scared. She knows regardless of what circumstances she faces in life, all things will work together for her good, for it is written!

A Boss Chick is a visionary. She can look past the rubbish of adversity and see the grand results that her experience will produce. Therefore, she doesn't allow insignificant things, people, or untimely events to hinder her growth. Instead, she becomes grateful for all her blessings and looks for the best out of life. She utilizes the fuel she gains from being thankful to push forward, especially during rainy seasons. Knowing bitterness is a heavy weight to carry, which clouds our judgment, modifies our character, and alters our goals, she avoids it at all costs! It is her wisdom that protects her and leads her to prosperity!

A Boss Chick doesn't take things others do personally. She understands as one of God's ambassadors here on earth, she will always be a target of her true enemy, Satan. Knowing his job is to steal, kill, and destroy, she recognizes he will use anyone as a pawn to derail her future. Therefore, a Boss Chick stays on top of her game! She is not ignorant of Satan's devices. She has been tested several times through life experiences, which have equipped her with vital insight. When people do unkind things, she quickly detaches herself. She doesn't allow them to distract her or take her off course. As a result, she retains her power and closes the door to unnecessary hardships.

A Boss Chick knows the detriment of unreleased anger and resentment. Bitterness produces the sin of un-forgiveness. Therefore, she does not wallow in these negative emotions because she knows they are door openers for self-destruction. When negative emotions arise, she addresses the root cause of them, and she makes a conscious effort to let them go. By doing so, a Boss Chick closes the door to negativity and protects her body from toxic emotions that cause illness.

A Boss Chick understands the power of forgiveness. She knows that as long as she stays angry with an individual, she will allow that person to become her jailor. Consequently, the pain they caused her will not cease. Every time she thinks of what the individual has done to her, she will experience pain, causing her to suffer even more. In contrast, when she forgives those who have wronged her, she allows room for God to step in and permanently heal her. Therefore, she makes a conscious effort not to remain angry. Instead, a Boss Chick utilizes forgiveness as her weapon to overcome adversity. As a result, she takes back her power from her abuser, heals, and triumphs in every area of her life!

A Boss Chick knows it is never wise to try to get even with others who cross her. She understands her covenant with God is her protection from evil. Therefore, no weapon formed (no matter how huge it may seem) against her will prosper, so she has no need to fear! Having this security allows her to remain peaceful, knowing God is her avenger. A Boss Chick understands if she attempts to take revenge herself, she will lose her covenant protection and place herself in harm's way. Therefore, she allows God to fight her battles, causing her enemies to become her footstools as she wins every war!

A true Boss Chick knows success is the best revenge. Therefore, she channels adversity into motivation, and she utilizes it to propel her to the top! Instead of being hateful to those who wish her harm, she stabs them with her kind words and a smile. As a result, she is constantly lifted up in the presence of her enemies, causing even those who hate her to recognize the anointing that lies on her life.

Knowing that adversity in life is unavoidable, and at times people will disappoint her, a Boss Chick uses her wisdom to overcome life's hardships. She implements these six powerful steps to healing, which helps to guard her heart from defilement:

STEP ONE (PRAY)

The first step to overcoming adversity is to pray. One simple prayer has the power to solve every problem you ever encounter. God is a gentleman. He will not get involved until you request His assistance. Therefore, in order to get results, PRAY!

Don't just pray for yourself, also pray for all those who have mistreated you. By praying for those who have wronged you, you will regain your power, giving you the strength to dethrone any negativity that has attempted to take root in your mind. Praying and leaving your cares in God's hands will give you ultimate peace and protection. You'll be surprised by the actions God takes on your behalf. Trust they will be greater than anything you could put together on your own!

STEP TWO (FORGIVENESS)

Forgiving those who wronged you will remove you from bondage and give you back your power. Never stay angry with those who harm you. It will only cause you further turmoil. Therefore, make a conscious effort to forgive!

STEP THREE (SILENCE)

Refuse to continue to talk about negative events that have affected you. After you pray, make peace with the situation and continue on your path. A Boss Chick knows less is more. No one should ever know your next move, especially your "haters"! Therefore, always keep on your poker face and don't let your mouth put you in harm's way. Remain silent and let God help you to secretly strategize your victory!

STEP FOUR (PRAISE/GRATITUDE)

If you ever want to confuse the enemy, make a conscious effort to rejoice! The happier you appear, especially after you have been wronged, the more confusion you will cause in the minds of your enemies. This is an essential strategy for natural and spiritual warfare. Therefore, think of all you have to be grateful for and REJOICE!!! As your praises go up, indeed your blessings will pour down!

STEP FIVE (PLAN FOR SUCCESS)

It is important you positively channel your energy to weed out all negativity. Therefore, broaden your scope by reading and writing. Challenge yourself by taking up hobby classes, or even going back to school to earn certificates or the degree you always wanted. Most importantly, set goals. See the bigger picture and plan to make it happen! By planning for success, even during adversity, you will position yourself to win!

STEP SIX (STAY FOCUSED)

By staying focused on your goals you will have no time to entertain bitterness. Your steady focus will help to thwart all the weapons of distraction your "haters" attempt to send, which will cause them further anger. Tunnel vision helps to manifest your greatest victory and will lift you up in the presence of your enemies. Therefore, strategize to win by remaining focused!

Staying prayed up and following these steps to healing will keep you on top of your game! For every enemy you defeat through spiritual wisdom, the more your power and virtue will increase for the world to see you are indeed a true Boss Chick!

WARNING!!!******If you allow yourself to become bitter you will miss out on your blessings. Bitterness will destroy your self-esteem and reflect in your behavior through unexpected mood swings, which will cause others to avoid you. A bitter person will be resistant toward helping others, ruining a crucial dynamic of becoming successful through team effort. She will also become a touchy, defensive, and draining individual, leading herself down the path of self-destruction. Therefore, avoid this fate at all cost! Don't let life's adversities make you bitter. Use them as fuel to make you BETTER!!!

PRACTICAL ANALYSIS

Every task we wish to accomplish on this earth requires energy. Energy is the spiritual substance that helps us to cultivate success. Without energy we cannot produce, find happiness, or obtain fulfillment. Therefore, it is essential that a Boss Chick discovers the outlet that fuels her energy. And she must guard it and not allow energy thieves to steal her fuel.

Energy is created by passion. When you find your passion you will discover your energy tank. In contrast, energy is sucked out by negativity. Energy thieves are those who are on assignment to rob your source of fuel. Any time we allow negativity into our lives, it drains our energy and steals our productivity. Therefore, the key to long-term success is to tap into your passion, find your fuel source, and guard it at all cost!

In this chapter, I will share a practical example of the detriment of allowing bitterness to take root in our lives and illustrate how you can turn negativity into motivation for success.

EXAMPLE ———

Keisha grew up in Charlotte, North Carolina. Her parents separated when she was 6 years old. Her mother remarried a wealthy businessman, Mr. Bob. After Keisha's mom, Ms. Pam, remarried, life took a sudden twist. Although the family had a picture-perfect look from the outside, living what appeared to be a wonderful life, the new family dynamics held dark secrets.

Mr. Bob was unattractive and significantly older than Ms. Pam. Tired of struggling to make ends meet, Ms. Pam knew Mr. Bob would be a great provider for her and her children. She was right! Mr. Bob moved the family into a big house and bought the children everything they could ever want. He particularly took a liking to Keisha. He would often fix her special meals and take her places.

Keisha was very fond of him too. Lacking the presence of her biological dad, she latched on to her new stepfather. In her mind, he was her hero.

All was well in Keisha's household . . . until she turned 12 years old. One night while she was sleeping, she was awakened when Mr. Bob's hands began to fondle her breasts. She tried to stop him, but his force was greater than her own. The man whom she thought was her hero ended up robbing her of her innocence.

Shocked and devastated by Mr. Bob's malicious actions, Keisha thought she could trust in her mother for comfort. To her dismay, her mother scolded her and rejected her accusations. From that moment on, everything went downhill for Keisha. Ms. Pam wanted nothing to do with her as she believed she was jeopardizing her family's life. Realizing he had the upper hand, Mr. Bob began to molest Keisha on a regular basis, with no remorse.

By the time Keisha turned 15, she ran away from home and severed all ties with her family. She found an older man to take care of her and moved in with him. Although this man was kind to Keisha and treated her well financially, she had no real affection toward him. She viewed him as a means to an end, got what she needed, and then left.

Throughout her adult life Keisha resented men. She blocked her heart and would not allow herself to love any of them. Consequently, they all became pawns in her game of life. One after another, she used and abused them, then tossed them to the side.

Not only did she cause these men pain, she also lived in turmoil. The bitterness in her heart caused her to be mean and nasty to those she interacted with, especially men. She was never able to settle down and be at peace. Constantly thinking about the abuse she suffered as a child, she disliked men in general, but particularly despised her stepfather. Repeating his vicious attacks in her mind helped to drain her energy and spiritual substance, leaving her void inside. The intensity of hate fueled her entire being, moving her to invoke the same affliction on others. Consequently, Keisha's bitterness led to illness. At the mere age of 27, she was diagnosed with cancer. Told she only had a short time to live, Keisha knew she would have to make peace with God.

After her diagnosis she joined a local church in her area where she met Sister Saunders, a devoted member of the church. Upon sharing her story with Sister Saunders, the woman of God was led to pray.

"Father God, we come to you in the mighty name of Jesus. The name higher than any other name. Lord, I intercede today on behalf of my dear sister Keisha. Lord, You know every problem and situation she has encountered and the turmoil she has endured in life. Father, Satan has tried to destroy her and rob her of her destiny, even as a small child. But, today, Lord, we declare that You are greater and more powerful than any plot of the enemy. Therefore, I utilize the authority that You have given me, and I bind every trap the enemy has designed over Keisha's life. I curse sickness and death that stand against her, and I declare she is a child of God whose life will now be used for your perfect purpose. Touch her heart, Lord, and heal her everywhere she hurts. Show her Your plan for her life and lead the way, Lord. May You be given all the praise, honor, and glory, in Jesus' mighty name we pray. Amen," Sister Saunders passionately prayed.

Tears began to roll down Keisha's face as she felt the power of the anointing from the prayer. Filled with conviction, Keisha dedicated her life to God as Sister Saunders taught her the power of forgiveness. Keisha did the necessary inner work and began her process by forgiving her mother and her stepfather. As she released her pain at the altar, her energy was revived. Sister Saunders taught Keisha how to become grateful and praise God to regain the strength she needed to triumph over her sickness. Keisha took her advice and changed her focus.

Overnight, drastic changes began to occur. At the clinic where Keisha received cancer treatment she met a young male intern whom she became very close with. Her entire healing process allowed her to take down her guard and love this man who was very fond of her. He helped her to enroll in school and the two became a couple.

Several years have passed, and today, Keisha is cancer-free. Discovering her passion to help others overcome adversity, she is an RN at the hospital she once received treatment from. And her husband, the young intern she met, is an oncologist at the same hospital. Keisha is also a Christian counselor at her church, where she ministers to many woman who encountered traumatic events in their lives. She helps them heal using the same steps Sister Saunders taught her.

Keisha's victory came when she learned to forgive and take back her power and energy. Today, bitterness no longer has a hold on her. She learned the secret of deliverance from bondage. Utilize life adversities as fuel to make you better!

JEWEL DROPS

- A Boss Chick is a woman who understands the true purpose of life's obstacles and uses them as motivation to move ahead. Instead of allowing adversity to make her bitter, she uses it as the driving force to make her better!
- Instead of attempting to avoid challenges that arise, a Boss Chick faces them head-on and takes the time out to discover the opportunity that lies within them. Her wisdom positions her to rejoice when others run scared! She knows regardless of what circumstances she faces in life, all things will work together for her good, for it is written!
- A Boss Chick is a visionary. She can look past the rubbish of adversity and see the grand results that her experience will produce. Therefore, she doesn't allow insignificant things, people, or untimely events to hinder her growth. Instead, she becomes grateful for all her blessings and looks for the best out of life.
- A Boss Chick doesn't take things that others do personally. She understands that as one of God's ambassadors

here on earth, she will always be a target of her true enemy, Satan. Knowing his job is to kill, steal, and destroy, she recognizes that he will use anyone as a pawn to derail her future. Therefore, she stays on top of her game!

- A Boss Chick knows the detriment of unreleased anger and resentment. Therefore, she does not wallow in these negative emotions because she knows they are door openers for self-destruction. When negative emotions arise, she addresses the issue that caused them, and makes a conscious effort to let them go. By doing so, she closes the door to negativity and protects her body from toxic emotions that cause illness.
- A Boss Chick understands the power of forgiveness. She knows that as long as she stays angry with an individual, she will allow that person to become her jailor. Consequently, the pain they caused her will not cease. In contrast, when she forgives those who have wronged her, she allows room for God to step in and permanently heal her wounds.
- A Boss Chick knows that it is never wise to try to get even with others that cross her. She understands that her covenant with God is her protection from evil. Therefore, no weapon formed (no matter how huge it may seem) against her will prosper, so she has no need to fear!
- A true Boss Chick understands success is the best revenge. Therefore she channels adversity into motivation, and she utilizes it to propel her to the top!

- A Boss Chick knows praise is a powerful weapon that will confuse her enemies! The happier she appears, especially after she's been wronged, the more confusion she will cause in the minds of her "haters." Additionally, God responds to the gratitude of His people. As her praises go up, indeed, her blessings will come pouring down!
- Energy is the spiritual substance that helps us to derive success. Without energy, we cannot produce, find happiness, or obtain fulfillment. Therefore, it is essential that a Boss Chick discovers the outlet that fuels her energy. And, she must guard it and not allow energy thieves to steal her fuel!

CHAPTER FIVE

Commandment V

"Thou Shall Not Allow Lust To Make You A Mother Before Love Makes You A Wife"

REVELATION

In today's society it is not uncommon for women to have children outside of marriage. Having a "baby's father" has become an acceptable norm. As a result, there are women raising children on their own, with little or no support from the men who helped to create them. Even more disheartening, we are giving birth to infants with no clue of their paternal bloodline. Consequently, some of us are independently raising kids whose lives are filled with chaos and turmoil stemming from generational curses.

Although it may be a hard fact to swallow, the sins of our forefathers result in curses on the family bloodline to the third and fourth generation. Simply said, if you choose to have a child with a murderer, the consequences of his sinful lifestyle may not only result in traumatic events for your child, but also your grandchildren, great-grandchildren, and great-great-grandchildren. This is real! Many of us are experiencing numerous difficulties with our children, without the understanding that they are suffering the repercussions of a family curse. Therefore, it is vital that before you consider allowing a man to father your child, not only should you check out his character, but also inquire of his ancestry. If not, your offspring may become victim to a family curse unless it is broken!

Raising a child is one of the most important functions of a woman, as we are created by God to reproduce. Our children represent our future genealogy. The morals and values we instill in them will have an effect for several generations to come. Understanding the importance of rearing a child and protecting your bloodline makes choosing a spouse a significant factor.

Children imitate the behavior of the parents who raised them. It is the parents who set the standards for what is and what is not acceptable behavior. Therefore, if you have babies out of wedlock, abuse alcohol, tolerate physical abuse from your significant other, collect public assistance as your financial plan for life, you set a precedent for your child to follow the same patterns. This principle is true in both spiritual and natural aspects. Think about how many people you know who have repeated the negative cycles of their parents. For instance, their mother was an alcoholic, and so was their grandmother. Now, the child battles with the same alcohol addiction. Some of the child's behavior may have been learned from the examples set for him or her, though this is not always the case.

There are many children who grow up in single-parent homes, raised by their mothers. Even though the child has no connection whatsoever with the father, he or she picks up the same negative traits as the absent parent. Many wonder, how this could be, when they never interacted. It is the sins of the forefather that now lie on the child. Spiritually, the child is drawn to the same adverse pattern of life as their father.

Understanding the critical nature of genealogy, it is important a Boss Chick not only raise her children with morals and set a good example, she must also wisely choose her child's father. He must be a man of integrity, who is committed to his family. Raising children must be just as important to this individual as it is to you. This kind of man will not be interested in having a "babies mother." Instead, he will seek after a wife to be the mother of his children.

Many women who battle with insecurity and abandonment issues attempt to trap men by becoming pregnant. They foolishly believe if they have this man's baby it will help the couple build a stronger bond. It is obvious in many cases this scheme does not work, yet women are still using this same tired tactic. When a woman truly loves herself, she does not seek to be kept by someone who doesn't want her. Attempting to manipulate the affection of a man when it is clear he has no real interest in you is a forbidden act. Attempting to control a man against his own will is dangerous, as it will surely backfire! When a man figures out he has been bamboozled, he will resent the woman and back away. In this case, the one who is left to suffer the most is the child who didn't ask to be brought into this world.

Children deserve the presence of a nurturing father figure in their lives. It is fathers who teach sons how to become men and show daughters what to expect from her king. Therefore, the absence of a father figure has great psychological effects on children. Knowing this fact, it is our duty, as mothers, to try to provide the most conducive environment for our children to flourish. This obligation takes place way before our child's conception. A Boss Chick thinks about the well-being of her future children way before they are born by only engaging in serious relationships with individuals who have the same morals and values as she does.

A Boss Chick takes dating seriously. She refuses to compromise her safety and the well-being of her offspring by engaging in risky sexual activity with men who lack stability and morals. Knowing her potential and her self-worth, she doesn't entertain individuals who are simply looking to have a good time on her dime. Protected by her standards, she guards herself from making a loser her "babies' daddy."

A Boss Chick knows the importance of commitment. Therefore, she does not latch on to individuals who do not wish to be kept. When she recognizes that a man lacks interest or fails to appreciate her, she does not reward him with sexual gratification. Instead, she makes a mindful choice to detach!

When a Boss Chick engages a man, she takes her time to find out about his interest, his values, and his family life. She watches how he treats his mother, sisters, and grandmother, and she uses that as a measure of how she can expect to be treated. A Boss Chick does not bite her tongue; she makes it her business to ask the men she chooses to date what they are looking for in a relationship. Dating gives her time to learn more about any potential mate. If a man shows a lack of interest in commitment, she does not put her life at risk by having unprotected sexual relations. Instead, a Boss Chick stays protected by dating those who share the same interest, morals, and family values. Knowing her high standards in advance, her boundaries ward off those who have commitment issues or lack integrity.

A Boss Chick refuses to play second to ANY woman. Therefore, she does not engage in sexual relationships with ANYONE else's boyfriend, fiancé, or husband. She honors marriage 100 percent and knows that a relationship with anyone but her own man will not work, because God simply will not "cosign" the relationship. Her wisdom teaches her "the same way you got that man will be the same way you lose that man." Knowing this truth, she does not put herself in compromising situations; she only dates those who honor her, claim her, and desire to be with her in a committed relationship.

A Boss Chick does not use her body as a tool to entrap a man. She desires a male companion who is attracted to her beauty, but also to her mind and personality. She understands that connecting with the mind, body, and soul is required to form a healthy compatible bond with her mate! Therefore, she doesn't attempt to bewitch a man through sex in order to keep him, because she knows it will not work!

A Boss Chick deserves a soul mate she can grow old with. Because of her desire for true companionship, she doesn't let lust make her settle with someone with whom she is not compatible. Knowing the value of marriage and the covenant protection it offers, a Boss Chick seeks out a husband, rather than a friend with "benefits."

A Boss Chick is a woman who refuses to allow lust to cloud her judgment. Before attempting to satisfy her flesh, she thinks ahead about the consequences of her actions. She knows a moment of pleasure is not worth a lifetime of grief. Therefore, she swiftly turns down enticing offers when she knows they stand to put her well-being at risk.

Having standards and setting boundaries makes a Boss Chick stand out to quality men who are attracted to her wholesome attributes. She knows a real king doesn't desire an imposter; he wants a queen, which is a woman of virtue. She is schooled to the fact men often test women when they are in search of a queen. If he sees a woman is willing to make "chickenhead" moves, he will disqualify her for the position as his wife; yet he may embrace her as his "side chick." Therefore, a Boss Chick passes his test with flying colors. Her integrity is the secret weapon that ultimately wins him over!

Regardless of how attractive or wealthy a man is, a Boss Chick is a woman who refuses to let her standards down. By raising the bar, she doesn't allow lust to make her a mother before love makes her a wife!

PRACTICAL ANALYSIS

A Boss Chick knows the difference between lust and love. Lust seeks temporary pleasure, while love seeks long-term companionship. Lust degrades one's self for a moment of satisfaction, while love seeks to endlessly build up and satisfy the one that it loves. When the sensation is over, lust fades away, yet love endures strenuous hardships, which results in stronger bonds.

In today's society, it is common for women to place an incorrect value on relationships based on lust. Instead of seeking long-term, compatible partnerships, women are chasing men who appeal to the eyes or their financial desires, yet lack integrity. Consequently, their misplaced pursuits cause severe turmoil, often resulting in a lifetime of pain, all which could have been avoided.

A Boss Chick doesn't just live for today. Her integral lifestyle requires her to keep tomorrow in mind. In this chapter, we will explore an example that will illustrate the detriment of being swayed by lust and the virtue of a relationship built on love and family values. It is my goal to enlighten you to the common repercussions of those who let temporary satisfaction blind them.

EXAMPLE ———

C.J. grew up in Baltimore, Maryland. As a child he always dreamed of being an entertainer. His love of poetry allowed him to escape from everyday life in the ghetto, as he would write for hours on the porch of his row house.

Gaining acceptance to the High School of Performing Arts, C.J. decided to pursue his dreams as a music major. At school, he was attracted to a pretty girl name Alicia. She had smooth caramel skin, hazel eyes, and a voluptuous body. Just thinking about Alicia inspired C.J. to write.

Highly sought after by several of the male students, Alicia didn't take much interest in C.J. Although he was also attractive, she felt she could do better, so she turned down his propositions.

Maria, a talented girl who moved from New York City to Baltimore, Maryland, was extremely attracted to C.J, who was her schoolmate. They often crossed paths and spoke for hours about their life experiences. Maria was also a pretty girl who C.J. was attracted to, but he quickly realized she was not willing to give up her "cookie" without real commitment.

C.J.'s passion for music led him to become a rapper. After being discovered by a talent scout who visited his school, C.J. was signed to a major recording label and given a hefty advance. While recording, C.J. was still able to complete school. Upon hearing he was signed, Alicia took sudden notice of him. Thrilled to be able to have the girl of his dreams, C.J. decided to make Alicia his girl.

After dropping his album, C.J.'s recording career took off. He became a Platinum-selling artist, winning multiple awards for his music. Alicia, scared she could lose C.J., decided she would get off of birth control and have a baby by him. She figured even if they didn't remain together she would be financially taken care of for the rest of her life.

Soon after stopping birth control, Alicia got pregnant. C.J. appeared to be happy at first, but after Alicia dropped out of school and became completely dependent on him, he began to have second thoughts.

As time passed, C.J.'s lust for Alicia disappeared. He now was in position to get any woman he wanted, so Alicia's beauty no longer appeased him. He became hooked on life in the fast lane. Every night he had a different woman of his choice, and he began drinking heavily. Introduced to heroin by one of his lady friends, C.J. became hooked. Within a few years he became a completely dysfunctional addict who could no longer meet the obligations of his record label, so his contract was terminated.

Alicia, left to raise little C.J. alone, was no longer handed large amounts of cash from her famous "baby daddy." With a limited education and few options, she believed she had no choice but to seek another male who could provide for her. One after another, men entered in—and out—of her life. Instead of working on improving herself, she continued to use her beauty and body to trap men. Consequently, she had three more children by three different men, who all ended up leaving her.

Her last child's father was a notorious drug dealer, known for murdering people who infringed on his drug turf. Alicia thought she finally found the man of her dreams—until he was arrested and sentenced to serve life in a federal penitentiary.

Today, Alicia's life is in a total shamble. She is a single mother, raising four children, who are all battling with issues. Young C.J. is a drug addict, just like his father and his grandfather. Her youngest child by her drug dealer boyfriend is currently in juvenile detention center for violently attacking a schoolmate who made a disrespectful joke about his mother. Her son stabbed his classmate three times in the neck.

At a recent high school reunion, Alicia reacquainted with Maria, who married her soul mate after she completed college. Although she dated several men, she stuck to her values. As a result, Maria's character attracted the man of her dreams, who is a prominent attorney. Maria and her husband have three beautiful children. Their oldest is a son, and they have two younger daughters. Maria's husband, Mike, participates in sports with his son, keeps him groomed nicely, and teaches him godly principles. Mike also showers his daughters with affection and teaches them they are valuable princesses who deserve to be loved and respected by men. Although everything is not always perfect in their household, their family values and morals keep the family on track.

After looking at Maria's life, Alicia questioned where she went wrong. The girls both started in the same exact place, with the same opportunities, yet their life circumstances worked out to be drastically different.

SUMMATION

Many women have been bamboozled by their fears and desire to be accepted. Blinded by what appears to be an enticing reward, these women have children with men they truly do not know.

I by no means am exempt from making mistakes. I had my son a year prior to marrying my husband. Later understanding the virtue of being married and raising a family, I had the ability to correct my error. Becoming a wife and raising our son together, I understand the importance of my husband in our lives. Where I fall short, he is there to lift me up. The endless hours he spends molding our son is nothing compared to what I could have done alone. Comparing my life growing up without a dad, to my son's life, I can clearly see the substantial differences and deficiencies I experienced. I missed out on a lot!

I urge every woman who has the desire to become a Boss Chick to set standards and boundaries. Don't think solely about pleasure or temporary gain. Look for long-term stability and prosperity for future generations to come. Therefore, don't let lust make you a mother before love makes you a wife!

JEWEL DROPS

- Although it may be a hard fact to swallow, the sins of our forefathers result in curses on the family bloodlines to the third and fourth generation. Therefore, it is vital that before you consider allowing a man to father your child, not only should you check out his character, but also inquire about his ancestry. If not, your offspring may become victim to a family curse unless it is broken!
- Raising a child is one of the most important functions of a woman, as we are created by God to reproduce. The morals and values we instill in them will have an effect for several generations to come. Understanding the importance of rearing a child and protecting your bloodline makes choosing a spouse a significant factor.
- There are many children who grow up in single-parent homes, raised by their mothers. Even though the child has no connection whatsoever to the father, he or she picks up the same negative traits as their absent parent. Many wonder, how this could be, when they never interacted. It is the sins of the forefathers that now lie on the child. Spiritually, the child is drawn to the same adverse pattern of life as their father.
- Understanding the critical nature of genealogy, it is important that a Boss Chick not only raises her children with morals and sets a good example, she must also wisely choose her child's father. He must be a man of integrity, who is committed to his family. Raising children must be

just as important to this individual as it is to you. This kind of man will not be interested in having a "baby's mother." Instead, he will seek after a wife to be the mother of his children.

- A Boss Chick does not seek to be kept by someone who doesn't want her. She knows attempting to manipulate the affection of a man, when it is clear he has no real interest in her, is a dangerous act, which will surely backfire! She understands when a man figures out he has been bamboozled he will resent her and back away, causing even more inner turmoil. Therefore, she only pursues individuals who genuinely desire her companionship.
- A Boss Chick takes dating seriously. She refuses to compromise her safety and the well-being of her offspring by engaging in risky sexual activity with men who lack stability and morals. Knowing her potential and her self-worth, she doesn't entertain individuals who are simply looking to have a good time on her dime. Protected by her standards, she guards herself from making a loser her "baby's daddy."
- When a Boss Chick engages a man she takes her time to find out about his interests, his values, and his family life. Dating gives her time to learn about any potential mate. She watches how he treats his mother, sisters, and grandmother, and she uses that as a measure of how she can expect to be treated.
- A Boss Chick refuses to play second to ANY woman. Therefore, she does not engage in sexual relationships

with ANYONE else's boyfriend, fiancé, or husband. She honors marriage 100 percent and knows that a relationship with anyone but her own man will not work, because God simply will not "cosign" the relationship. Knowing this truth, she does not put herself in compromising situations; she only dates those who honor her, claim her, and desire to be with her in a committed relationship.

- A Boss Chick is a woman who refuses to allow lust to cloud her judgment. Before attempting to satisfy her flesh she thinks ahead about the consequences of her actions. She knows a moment of pleasure is not worth a lifetime of grief. Therefore, she swiftly turns down enticing offers when she knows they stand to put her well-being at risk.
- Having standards and setting boundaries makes a Boss Chick stand out to quality men who are attracted to her wholesome attributes. She knows a real king doesn't desire an imposter; he wants a queen, which is a woman of virtue. She is schooled to the fact men often test women when they are in search of a queen. If he sees a woman is willing to make "chickenhead" moves, he will disqualify her for the position as queen, yet he may embrace her as his "side chick." Therefore, a Boss Chick passes his test with flying colors. Her integrity is the secret weapon that ultimately wins him over!

CHAPTER SIX

Commandment VI

"Thou Shall Save Money, And Money Will Save You"

REVELATION

A Boss Chick understands the importance of money. Recognizing its value she doesn't spend it frivolously, nor does she take for granted viable opportunities to increase her wealth. She acknowledges money as the instrument that will not only cover her basic expenses, but will also reward her with material luxuries and fund her imagination. With it, she can empower others through her giving and live a prosperous life. Without it, she will live in poverty and lack. Therefore, there is no question that every Boss Chick needs money to flourish and conquer her dreams. It is her ability to save money and make it grow that makes her a standout amongst her peers!

Although a Boss Chick values currency, she does not place a higher value on it then it deserves. She knows it is God who gives her the ability to obtain wealth. It is the anointing He places on her life that gives her wisdom and insight and draws prosperity to her. Therefore, a Boss Chick does not honor money over God, nor does she lust after it. Her wisdom protects her from self-destruction, for she knows "the love of money is the root of all evil!"

A Boss Chick is a woman of integrity who guards her reputation. She pays all her debts on time and does not make purchases that will threaten her financial stability. As a result, she maintains good credit and uses it moderately to further build her wealth.

A Boss Chick understands that bad debt has the power to hinder her progress. Therefore, she refuses to fall victim to its fiery reigns. Knowing that many others are debt's victims who work solely to pay their bills, she avoids this fate at all costs! Instead of trying to keep up with the Joneses, she doesn't squander money on frivolous things; she makes purchases in allotments she can afford. By doing so, she avoids wearing an expensive dress today that she'll pay five times the price for over the next 3 years, when the dress is no longer in style.

A Boss Chick doesn't live just for today, she always keeps tomorrow in mind. She is an independent woman who does not rely on the finances of others to support her. Therefore, she takes time out to develop a savings and retirement plan which will keep her flourishing in the future.

A Boss Chick never spends all of her earnings, nor does she live "paycheck to paycheck." Off the top, she devotes 10 percent of her gross earnings to God, by paying her tithes. Knowing it is He who gives her the power to obtain wealth, she offers Him the firstfruits of her earnings. As a result, God honors her and blesses her with more. He shields her with His covenant protection, and she always has surplus!

After a Boss Chick pays her tithes, she takes out at least another 10 percent to go toward her savings plan, leaving a maximum of 80 percent of her available income to spend. A Boss Chick does not simply bury her savings in a bank account or underneath her bed. She recognizes the fact that "it takes money to make money," so she utilizes her wealth to create more. She invests her income in a higher-interest rate money market and certificate of deposit accounts, as well as stocks, bonds, and mutual funds. She takes time out to research profitable investments. As a result, she becomes a wise steward over her wealth and watches her money steadily grow!

A Boss Chick understands the difference between assets and liabilities. She knows liabilities will only cost her money, yet will not appreciate her net worth, so she avoids these "financial booby traps." In an effort to increase her net worth, a Boss Chick makes it a priority to increase her assets. Knowing the value of purchasing land and real estate, a Boss Chick seeks out valuable investments. Her wisdom leads her to become a home owner, rather than a renter. As a result, instead of depreciating her wealth by renting, she'd rather appreciate her net worth by increasing the equity in the home she owns. Not only does she establish wealth for herself, she builds a substantial portfolio that passes down to her children and grandchildren, creating an empire that lasts for generations to come!

A Boss Chick knows the importance of residual income. Therefore, she seeks out investments that will give her a monthly, quarterly, and yearly return. Not only does she endeavor to become a home owner, she also plans to hold the title of landlord. As a result, she collects additional monthly cash flow and builds equity in her investment properties using OPM (other people's money). This wise tactic helps her to establish more wealth. By the time she reaches retirement age, she owns several properties debt free and is able to use her rental income to finance her dreams.

A Boss Chick is a woman who utilizes her money to take advantage of good business opportunities. She realizes that she will never become wealthy by simply working for someone else. Therefore, she finds ways to become her own boss. Girded with money, she finds prosperous business ventures that help her employ others; at the same time, she grows her net worth.

A Boss Chick is a woman who believes in giving back. She does not hoard her wealth for just herself or her family. A Boss Chick donates her time and her money to support worthy charitable causes. By giving back, she funnels money and resources to worthy missions, empowering others to overcome life's hardships. The satisfaction she gains from her contributions are not only self-fulfilling, they cause the universe to increase her wealth!

A Boss Chick is a woman who has a secure retirement plan, which includes Individual Retirement Accounts (IRA), a 401(k) plan, or Keogh accounts. She divides her retirement savings into safe investment accounts which yield higher returns. She utilizes this money as her safety net, contributing to her fund on a regular basis. As a result, she gets pleasure in watching her money grow, and she rests safely knowing her future is secure!

A Boss Chick knows having insurance is vital. Therefore, she maintains quality life, health, auto, and homeowners insurance. If she rents a dwelling, she maintains rental insurance as well. By doing so, she plans ahead to be protected in the event hardships arise. Having this protection gives her a sense of ease and guards her empire.

A Boss Chick is a woman who knows "rainy seasons" will come. Understanding this truth, she takes her time and builds her house on solid ground, not sand. Taking note of the lesson behind the old fable "The Three Little Pigs," when the big bad wolf of life's obstacles occurs with the power to blow her house down, she is protected! The strong brick and mortar of her foundation keeps her house standing, while she watches others who built their house with sticks wash away. A Boss Chick's experiences teach her that as long as she saves her money, her money will save her!

PRACTICAL ANALYSIS

If you want to be powerful, influential, and help others, it will require you to have money. Many people become stagnated in life because they believe it's too hard to acquire wealth, but that just isn't true!

In this chapter, I will give you a snippet of my personal life and an example of how securing savings, making the right decisions, and scouting out financial opportunities can give you the ability to build your empire from scratch . . . and maintain it. I am a living example that a "project chick," as some may call me, can independently break the bonds of poverty. My story will share insight on strategies that contributed to my success.

At a young age, I was taught the importance of saving money. Watching my single mother budget money in an effort to make ends meet, I learned the value of saving for a "rainy day." My father was absent from our lives emotionally, physically, and financially. Therefore, my mother had no choice but to budget. She was very disciplined with the little she had, making sure we always had the essentials we needed. I always respected and admired that. As a little girl, I intensely watched her work hard and save money to provide a better life for us.

I got my first job at McDonald's when I was 15 years old. My mother made me a proposition I could not refuse. She said if I saved $500, she would match my money and help me open my first savings account. I was eager to accomplish this goal, so I saved as much as I could from each paycheck until I had my $500 in hand.

I'll never forget the day I walked into the Dime Savings Bank in Green Acres Mall, located in Valley Stream, New York. With my mother by my side, we opened my first passbook savings account. I handed the bank teller my money, and she looked at my mom with a puzzled look. Instantly, my mom blurted out to the bank teller, "I am teaching my only child the importance of managing her finances. She has to learn to save her money, so her money can save her."

On the ride home, my mother gave me a long lecture about the value of money and what it could help me accomplish. She made it clear to me that wasting my money on unnecessary material items would hinder my growth. The passion in her voice and the urgency in her tone made me take heed to her words. At that moment, I knew if I desired to be successful in life, I needed to learn how to make as much money as I could and save it!

Following the pattern that was set for me, I saved up my money the entire time I was employed at McDonald's. At 15 years old, I started out as a cashier, and within 3 years I advanced to assistant manager. At 17 years old, I was accepted to John Jay College. My freshman year, financial aid helped fund my education. But after my spring semester, I was no longer eligible for assistance. It was my savings from my job that helped me fund my education. Without it, I would have been stuck!

Although many years have passed since I opened my first savings account, the principles I learned from saving money have saved me on several occasions. Without money, I wouldn't have been able to make the investments that increased my wealth so substantially, which put me in position to own several thriving businesses. My experience has taught me maintaining good credit and savings is essential for a Boss Chick to create an empire.

Making money alone will not sustain you. If you do not invest your money wisely, it will disappear! I want to share with you an example of two sisters who both started out with a substantial allotment of money, but the results of their investments ended drastically different.

EXAMPLE ———

Tiffany and Angela are two sisters who grew up in Long Island City, New York. Their father was a courageous firefighter who lost his life in the World Trade Center during the 9/11 crisis.

Both girls were in college during the time their dad passed. Given a little over $500,000 apiece, Tiffany decided to quit college and take time off to grieve. Angela, who was a few semesters from completing her bachelor's degree in psychology, became consumed in her studies to keep her mind off the tragic event that had occurred.

Upon receiving her inheritance, Tiffany opened up a Money Market Savings account, where she was able to obtain a higher interest rate on her money without committing it for any locked period of time. She immediately began to travel the country as a means to escape her pain. As time went by, she enjoyed the ability to go where she wanted, any time she desired. As a result, her traveling became more frequent. She ventured to every continent in the world, exploring different cultures.

Angela urged Tiffany to buy a house, but she decided against it. She liked her freedom of escaping whenever she chose to, and she didn't want the responsibility of maintaining a home.

On the other hand, Angela took her money and invested half of it in certificate of deposit accounts, which were FDIC insured. She also used some money to purchase a home to live in, and a four-family rental property. Her wise investment brought her an immediate return. With the positive cash flow she gained from her rental property, she paid both of her monthly mortgage notes and she still had cash left over each month.

After completing her bachelor's degree, Angela worked under a psychologist for 2 years. While employed, she reenrolled in college and received her master's degree in psychology. After graduating, she used the interest she gained from her investments to start her own private practice.

Watching the real estate market, Angela found two more investment properties at a very good price. Realizing that investing in real estate would give her a better return than her certificate of deposit accounts, she cashed her CDs and bought the two investment properties outright. As a result, she earned triple the amount of money she previously made on interest. With the extra money she made from rentals, Angela invested in mutual funds, which earned her a steady return at a high interest rate. Within 5 years after receiving her inheritance, Angela became a multimillionaire. The properties she purchased had almost doubled in value during the real estate boom, and her wise financial investments procured her very high returns.

On the other hand, 5 years after receiving her settlement, Tiffany was down to her last $50,000. Believing her inheritance was so large that it would never diminish, she squandered her money frivolously. Today, the only tangible items Tiffany has from her inheritance are her memories and pictures of places she traveled to. She now regrets her financial decisions. By looking at her sister's investment decisions, she realizes that assets last while memories fade away.

Tiffany is currently reenrolled back in college at age 32, with the hope her education will help her resurrect her former lifestyle. While she is finally working on obtaining her associate's degree, her sister Angela is now pursuing her Ph.D.

JEWEL DROPS

- A Boss Chick understands the importance of money. Recognizing its value she doesn't spend it frivolously nor does she take for granted viable opportunities to increase her wealth.

- Although a Boss Chick values currency, she does not place a higher value on it then it deserves. She knows it is God who gives her the ability to obtain wealth. Therefore, she does not honor money over God, nor does she lust after it.
- A Boss Chick is a woman of integrity who guards her reputation. She pays all her debts on time and does not make purchases that will threaten her financial stability.
- A Boss Chick understands that bad debt has the power to hinder her progress. Therefore, she refuses to fall victim to its fiery reigns. Knowing that many others are debt's victims who work solely to pay their bills, she avoids this fate at all costs!
- A Boss Chick doesn't live just for today. She always keeps tomorrow in mind. She is an independent woman who does not rely on the finances of others to support her. Therefore, she takes time out to develop a savings and retirement plan, which will keep her flourishing in the future.
- A Boss Chick never spends all of her earnings, nor does she live "paycheck to paycheck." Off the top, she devotes 10 percent of her gross earnings to God by paying her tithes. Knowing it is He who gives her the power to obtain wealth, she offers him the firstfruits of her earnings. As a result, God honors her and blesses her with more. He shields her with His covenant protection, and she always has surplus!

- A Boss Chick does not simply bury her savings in a bank account or underneath her bed! She recognizes the fact that "it takes money to make money," so she utilizes her wealth to create more.
- In an effort to increase her net worth, a Boss Chick makes it a priority to increase her assets. Her wisdom leads her to become a home owner, rather than a renter. As a result, instead of depreciating her wealth by renting, she'd rather appreciate her net worth by increasing the equity in the home she owns.
- A Boss Chick knows the importance of residual income. Therefore, she seeks out investments that will give her a monthly, quarterly, and yearly return. Not only does she endeavor to become a home owner, she also plans to hold the titles of investor and landlord.
- A Boss Chick is a woman who believes in giving back. She does not hoard her wealth for just herself or her family. A Boss Chick donates her time and her money to support worthy charitable causes. By giving back, she funnels money and resources to worthy missions, empowering others to overcome life's hardships.

CHAPTER SEVEN

Commandment VII

"Thou Shall Allow Teamwork To Make The Dream Work"

REVELATION

Every successful kingdom or empire requires the joint effort of a team. When we come together in unity, on one accord, nothing is impossible! Each of us was created with different gifts and talents that complement one another. A Boss Chick is a woman who has the wisdom to align herself with key individuals who help refine and complement her gifts. She understands the value of these alliances, so she honors and nurtures them. As a result, a Boss Chick builds a powerful team around her that works together to accomplish her purpose on earth.

A Boss Chick is a multifaceted woman who knows her position well, no matter what capacity is required. Although she often plays the role of a star player on the team, she realizes at times it's healthy to sit on the bench and cheer her teammates on. With ease, she takes advantage of opportunities to dunk the ball; yet, she still makes effective passes, allowing those around her a chance to score. Most importantly, a Boss Chick doesn't think she knows everything! She surrounds herself with wise counsel, and she takes heed to her coach's advice. As a result, not only does she win great levels of accomplishment, so does her entire team!

A Boss Chick understands the principle that there is no "i" in team. She is not self-centered, nor does she promote causes that are strictly beneficial to herself. She is a woman of integrity that knows her purpose on earth is to benefit society. Therefore, she attracts those with similar assignments, and they work jointly to complete their mission.

A Boss Chick is a visionary and an inspiring leader. She effectively communicates her plans to her teammates, and she strategically delegates assignments according to the skill sets and talents that each team member possesses. Up front, she lets these individuals know what she expects and the time frame in which to deliver. Prior to starting the assignment, she also requires these individuals to communicate back to her their understanding of her expectations. This dialogue helps keep her team informed and on the same page.

A Boss Chick not only delegates duties to others, she also rolls up her sleeves and takes an active role in team efforts. It is her passion and energy that inspires her entire team to reach their goals. Not only does she fuel herself, she looks for opportunities to compliment team players and makes efforts to help them improve their craft.

When a Boss Chick is successful at a group task, she does not take all the credit. She recognizes the hard work of all the individuals involved in the project, and she compensates them well for their contributions. Her genuine appreciation and loyalty motivates her team to work harder and excel even greater. As a result, her empire continues to grow!

A Boss Chick is not only a team player at her job, she is also a team player at home. She honors and respects her king and works jointly with him to maintain their kingdom. A Boss Chick never neglects the duties of a wife. She works intensely to ensure her king is satisfied. As the head of the palace, she listens closely to his desires and helps him to fulfill them. As a result, she continues to be held in great esteem of her king, who honors and respects her greatly. Although she is often busy handling other matters, she always sets aside quality time to spend with her king. She is loving, kind, and affectionate toward him, pampering her king with her virtuous qualities. She makes a conscious effort to be open and understanding, lending her ear during his times of need.

A Boss Chick is never judgmental, nor is she defensive. Instead, she tries her best to understand her mate's point of view. And if she doesn't, she respectfully explains her position and asks for clarification to gain further insight. Instead of jumping to conclusions, she uses communication as a means to settle her discontentment. She does not nag, irritate, or force her king to be someone he is not. Instead, she sets the ground rules of what she expects as his wife, and works with her king to satisfy this expectation.

A Boss Chick is committed to the success of her team. When times get rough or problems arise, she stays grounded for the long haul. Understanding the value of those whom she relies on, she makes an effort to be patient and understanding. Her genuine care and compassion causes those who work with her to become wholeheartedly committed to their mission. As a result, her support system remains grounded and attracts others who wish to join the alliance.

A Boss Chick is a peacemaker. She does not instigate gossip or stir up trouble. Instead, she works vigorously to put out fires and takes measure to prevent them. By discouraging internal competition and keeping her team focused on their goals, she is able to maintain peace in her workplace and her home. For she knows once she allows any negativity, it will breed further discourse. Therefore, she nips it in the bud, at the root!

By honoring, valuing, and showing loyalty to her team, a Boss Chick has great success and maintains longevity in her relationships. She knows it is not her independent effort that makes her a boss. Experience has taught this virtuous woman teamwork makes the dream work!

NOTICE******Some may say they do not need a team to be a successful, believing they can obtain better results on their own. The truth is, you are only as powerful as the team that supports you. Individually, your potential will always be limited. With the assistance and insight of others, you can generally gain greater results and accomplish your task with less effort. God forbid you experience a challenge that limits your health or abilities; if you work by yourself you may be stuck! On the other hand, even if the leader of a strong team perishes, her legacy lives on in the strength of the team she developed!

PRACTICAL ANALYSIS

When I first started out in business, I had the attitude I could do everything on my own. Instead of hiring others to assist me, I figured I would save myself time and headaches by doing it all myself. Quickly, things became overwhelming. I worked night and day to accomplish tasks that would have taken a team a few hours to complete. Taking the advice of a few wise mentors, I decided to get help. This ultimately made my life easier and helped me achieve greater success.

At first, I would delegate duties to others and find myself either micromanaging them or taking back the task to perform myself. I had the mentality that no one could do things as well as I could, so I always took charge. Although my business sustained itself and covered my expenses, it wasn't until I developed leadership skills that my enterprise began to flourish.

I learned how to communicate my vision to employees, explain what I expected, and taught them how I would like them to achieve the desired results. As I became more efficient with managerial and interpersonal skills, I was able to motivate those whom I hired to perform at their best. As time went on, we developed a level of trust. I took pride in finding out about the things that affected them and what they enjoyed. Instead of just focusing on business, we also formed a personal bond. This bond helped me to create a loyal team who was committed to the success of the business. To date, I have many of the same riders on my team. Just like me, they play to win!

In 2009, I was blessed to marry my soul mate. I had prior experience in relationships and business, but I had no clue how to be a wife. As a woman of color in a generation that has devalued the sanctity of marriage, I had few resources to draw from. Through the struggles of life's trials and tribulations, experience has taught me vital steps to maintaining a healthy marriage. I learned the hard way, it also takes teamwork to make the marriage dream work!

Anyone who knows me can attest I am an outspoken woman who is passionate about what I believe in. I am the type that says what I mean and means what I say, no matter who I come in contact with. As a result, when I entered my marriage I would often challenge my husband's decisions and make plans without considering his input. This caused problems in our relationship. It wasn't until I began to familiarize myself with the Bible that I learned how to become a virtuous woman and a loving wife. I suggest any woman who wishes to do the same read Proverbs 31:10–31. The attributes described in this scripture depict a formula for an ultimate Boss Chick!

When a woman and man unite with one another they are no longer separate in the spirit. In God's eyes they become one. Therefore, wives are a reflection of their husbands, and husbands are a reflection of their wives. Together, they align as a team and work in union to achieve their goals. Instead of backbiting, competing, and degrading one another, married couples should uplift, cover, and protect each other.

I created an acronym for the word COUPLE: closeness, openness, understanding, peacemaking, loyalty, and esteem. These qualities uphold the marriage dream! They are the attributes a Boss Chick needs to possess to sustain a healthy marriage, which I will describe in more detail below:

CLOSENESS—Intimacy is a great part of marriage. Your husband should not only be your lover, he should also become your best friend. He is the one individual who you should desire to talk to and share your most intimate thoughts and dreams with. You should prioritize spending time with him. Never become too busy to please your man! Hold hands and take a walk, hug, kiss, pamper, and make love to each other. Whatever you do, refuse to lose your zeal! Keep your relationship hot, passionate, and spicy! Find out your mate's deepest desires and try your best to fulfill them.

Leave him wanting more and you won't have to worry about losing what he'll work hard to keep—your union!

OPENNESS- No intimate relationship will succeed without honesty and trust. Many make the mistake of pretending or keeping what they feel inside in an effort to sustain the esteem of their partner. Wrong move! Eventually, you will get tired of living a lie or "walking on egg shells." Therefore, it is important to be true to who you are and be open with your mate. When things occur that you do not like, talk about it. Fearlessly share your plans, dreams and desires, and allow your partner to help you fulfill them. By being open you will build trust in your relationship and be free to be yourself!

UNDERSTANDING—It's your job as a wife to be understanding. Husbands desire a woman whom they can share their feelings with, who'll be nonjudgmental, affectionate, and understanding. Don't feel you always have to interject; learn how to become your husband's listening ear, one who allows him to vent and share his concerns. Power couples have no room to be selfish. Therefore, always keep in mind the feelings of your lover and your relationship will flourish!

PEACEMAKING—A Boss Chick is the author of peace. She makes her best effort to keep the atmosphere in her home warm, comfortable, and peaceful, by quickly dissolving arguments and disagreements with her kind words of wisdom. When problems arise that are too hard for her to solve, she takes them to God in prayer. She asks Him for the strength she needs to contain her temperament, and gains endurance to resist the urge to argue with her spouse. She doesn't just pray by herself; she also prays with her husband and her children. Her wisdom teaches her, "a family that prays together stays together." Staying true to this principle, God answers her petitions each time she takes them to His throne.

LOYALTY—A Boss Chick understands the importance of loyalty. She is dedicated and 100 percent loyal to her husband and her children. Her loyalty doesn't just keep her free from infidelity, it also guards the reputation of those she loves.

A virtuous wife keeps her family business in her home. She does not share her family secrets with outsiders who may use this information against her or against those she loves. Instead, when problems arise, she makes it a point to settle each dispute within her own household.

A Boss Chick does not engage in relationships or take part in activities that her husband is unaware of. She openly shares her daily life with her spouse and allows him to be a part of her plans. As a result, she forms a strong bond with her husband, and they work together as a dream team!

ESTEEM—It is the job of a virtuous wife to build the esteem of her husband. She knows that behind every powerful man is a strong woman. Therefore, she makes it her business to uplift her man. She is the one who helps him identify his strengths and encourages him to excel. When he loses his drive or becomes frustrated, it is her warm words that strengthen him and motivates him to carry on.

A Boss Chick is a bright light to her husband. Through her reflection she helps him shine. Together, they become a power couple who inspire others to follow their path. With each other's support, they are unstoppable! When you see one, you can clearly see the reflection of the other. It is strength, unity, and loyalty that creates the bond which holds them tightly together. Even when times get rough they hold true to their vows, and they remain each other's best support. These are the qualities that empower a Boss Chick and her spouse to build a mighty empire!

Now that I have shared tips of a power couple, I encourage you to implement them into your own relationship. But let me warn you it takes time and practice to master these principles. Learning to become submissive to my husband and allowing him to be the head of my home hasn't been easy for me because of my past independent personality. But it works! The more I have made it a priority to build our closeness, become understanding, be a peacemaker, practice loyalty, and build his esteem, I have watched our marriage bond increase tremendously. I had to learn—just like in business, marriage requires teamwork to make the dream work too!

Below, I will share a practical example of a woman who encompasses the attributes described in this chapter. How she balances her life illustrates how it takes team effort to live a prosperous life.

EXAMPLE ———

Christina is the CEO and founder of a thriving health food chain. After graduating from college, she met her husband Ted, and they decided to save up and open their first store. The process wasn't easy as Ted had to work two jobs to create extra income to fund their project. When they saved up enough money, Ted quit both of his jobs to manage the store full-time. During that period it was very rough for the couple who had depended on a portion of Ted's income to make ends meet. Christina was determined to make their dream work, so she picked up her second job to cover their expenses.

Christina and Ted worked relentlessly, with hopes their investment would pay off. Although the couple was not able to spend as much time together, their dedication to each other increased. United, they strived hard to achieve their goals.

Within a year of opening the first store the business began to bloom. Christina was able to quit her jobs and began working at the store alongside her husband. They were also able to hire several employees. Ted handled the management of the store, while Christina spearheaded the marketing. She utilized the knowledge learned in college to promote the business, and it quickly began to grow. Recognizing the potential profitability of opening another store, Christina created store policies that helped structure the business even more. Each employee was assigned specific tasks and instructed on how to perform them. Christina broke down every aspect of the business and organized it in such a way that even a 17-year-old child could run the store.

As a result of her new system, Ted and Christina were able to open a second store with ease. The couple remained loyal to their original employees, promoting these individuals to higher positions as the business expanded. Creating a family-friendly environment for their employees that rewards them with bonuses and good benefits, their employees remain dedicated to the store and committed to the couple's dream.

After opening the third store, Christina gave birth to their first child, a little boy. While out on maternity leave, Ted gladly covered his wife's duties at the company. Christina stayed at home and took care of their son for the first 3 months. Then she was able to hire a babysitter to assist with child care so she could return to work.

Christiana works full-time at the health store. After a full day of work, she comes home and takes care of her son. Although her plate is full, she never neglects spending quality time with her husband. Once a week they set aside time to go out to eat and visit a place of their choice. Ted isn't just her spouse, he is also her best friend. The couple confides in each other; and when times get rough, they encourage each other.

Today, Ted and Christiana own five thriving health food stores, and they are currently looking to expand. The couple is committed to teaching minorities how to reduce obesity, stay healthy, and physically fit. Their efforts have resulted in nationwide recognition for their company. This fall, they are scheduled to receive an award for top fitness and health company of the year. Ted and Christina are respected by many. They have shown their peers the essence of a true power couple!

JEWEL DROPS

- Every successful kingdom or empire requires the joint effort of a team. When we come together in unity, on one accord, nothing is impossible.
- A Boss Chick is a multifaceted woman who knows her position well, no matter what capacity is required. With ease, she takes advantage of opportunities to dunk the ball, yet still makes effective passes, allowing those around her a chance to score.
- When a Boss Chick is successful at a group task, she does not take all the credit. She recognizes the hard work of all individuals involved in the project, and she compensates them well for their contributions. Her genuine appreciation and loyalty motivates her team to work harder, and her empire continues to grow.
- A Boss Chick never neglects her duties as a wife. She works intensely to ensure her king is satisfied. As the head of the palace, she listens closely to his desires and helps him to fulfill them. As a result, she continues to be held in great esteem by her king, who honors and respects her greatly.

- A Boss Chick is committed to the success of her team. When times get rough or problems arise, she stays grounded for the long haul. Understanding the value of those whom she relies on, she makes an effort to be patient and understanding. As a result, her support system remains grounded and attracts others who wish to join the alliance.
- A Boss Chick is a peacemaker. She does not instigate gossip or stir up trouble. Instead, she works vigorously to put out fires and takes measures to prevent them. By discouraging internal competition and keeping her team focused on their goals, she is able to maintain peace in her workplace and her home.
- A Boss Chick understands the importance of loyalty. She is dedicated and 100 percent loyal to her husband and her children. Her loyalty doesn't just keep her free from infidelity, it also guards the reputation of those she loves.
- A Boss Chick keeps her family business in her home. She does not share her family secrets with outsiders who may use this information against her or against those she loves. Instead, when problems arise, she makes it a point to settle each dispute within her own household.
- A Boss Chick does not engage in relationships or take part in activities that her husband is unaware of. She openly shares her daily life with her spouse and allows him to be a part of her plans. As a result, she forms a strong bond with him and they work together as a team!

- A Boss Chick is a bright light to her husband. Through her reflection she helps him shine. Together, they become a power couple who inspire others to follow their path. With each other's support, they are unstoppable!

CHAPTER EIGHT

Commandment VIII

"Thou Shall Not Compromise Your Self-Worth For Net Worth"

REVELATION

We live in a society where money and materialism are often valued over integrity and principles. Chasing after the "almighty dollar," many have sold their bodies and even their souls in an effort to gain what they perceived to be success. Some have accomplished their mission, obtaining great wealth and even superstardom, only to feel void inside. Think about how many rich celebrities, or people of great stature, commit suicide at the height of their careers. This illustrates that money, prestige, and material items alone are not enough to obtain peace or happiness.

As we previously discussed, a woman does not find real fulfillment until she discovers her true purpose on earth. To find your purpose, you must first tap into your passion. The very thing that you can do for hours without becoming bored and benefits mankind is most likely attached to your purpose. Until you take time to find out your assignment, life will be baseless and you will always feel as though you are missing out on something.

It's important to understand that your assignment on earth is merely temporary. It is simply preparation for eternal life, which will far exceed your present life conditions. It is my belief we are rewarded in our afterlife based on our performance during this earthly trial run. If you also believe that to be the case, then it is important to live your life with integrity and endeavor to make a sizable contribution to society during your lifetime. If today was your very last day on this earth, can you honestly say that God would look down upon you and feel you have fulfilled your destiny? If not . . . It's time to make some changes!

As a Boss Chick, it's important to live every day as if it's your last. There is no time for games when there is work to be done! A Boss Chick doesn't make plans for merely survival; she plans to leave behind a legacy that will last for many generations to come. In order to accomplish her goal, she knows she cannot compromise her self-worth for net worth, because that is a sure path of self-destruction!

There are many of us who devalue ourselves because we have no clue who we truly are, nor do we understand our spiritual value. A Boss Chick knows she is a tri-part being, who was made in the image of her Almighty Father. She is a spirit being, who lives in a body and possesses a soul. Unlike animals and other creatures who occupy this earth, not only do we live in a body and possess a soul, we are also living sprits. After our soul and body die, our spirit still lives on. It is our spirit that makes us unique and enables us to communicate directly with God, for we worship Him in spirit. Each of us possesses the ability to utilize our spirits to connect with our Creator. He speaks to us through a still small voice that some refer to as intuition. Have you ever got the feeling you shouldn't go down a certain path, and you followed that gut feeling, to later find out it was the best decision you have ever made? That was God talking to you! When we are in tune with Him, He protects us!

Distractions are used to blind and derail us. The spirit of lust is used to lure us into sin. Accepting the bait puts us at risk of forfeiting divine destiny or purpose, because sin is the destructive element that causes us to disconnect ourselves from God. Some lust after material items or money. Others lust after a high or sexual gratification. Whatever our weakness is, Satan will discover it and try to use it to destroy us. Subsequently, it is imperative a Boss Chick stay on top of her game and avoid self-destruction!

The enemy has many of us brainwashed. Chasing after material wealth and gratification, we become willing to compromise our values to receive superficial success. Following this pattern, many of us are stuck in bondage due to our immoral choices which have disconnected us from our true source—God. Only if we would have known the value of our spiritual connection and the importance of obtaining eternal life, we might not have let the cares of this world suck us dry. Fortunately for us, life is not over, so we each have an opportunity to change our course. Don't let a few moments of pleasure or temporary wealth jeopardize you from receiving eternal life. Instead, protect yourself by staying true to your integrity!

A Boss Chick's body is her temple. It is the place where God resides. Knowing its value, she takes care of her body and does not defile it. No matter how rough times may seem to get, she never sells her body for temporary gain or pleasure. She stands firm on this principle. As a result, she is honored and respected!

A Boss Chick is not willing to go against her moral code to gain the esteem or finances of another being. She does not look to man to take care of her needs because she knows that God Almighty is her provider.

A Boss Chick refuses to be a slave to any man, job, or organization. She does not let others make decisions for her, nor does she follow plans that have potential to cause her harm.

A Boss Chick is a free spirit who is led by God. Therefore, she refuses to allow people, places, or things to become her jailor.

A Boss Chick is a woman who pursues the path of a career versus a job. She knows a career will uplift her and lead her into her purpose, whereas a job is only a means to procure a paycheck. By pursuing her dreams she finds the thing she loves to do that will sustain her, enable her to give back to society, and bring her joy. As a result, she is successful in her field of choice and she prospers!

A Boss Chick is happy with the image she sees when she looks at her reflection in the mirror. She can walk the streets comfortably, without having to watch over her shoulder. She is a virtuous woman who feels good about herself and the choices she has made in life, so she is full of joy and self-confidence. She has sown many good seeds, so she stands firmly with expectancy of her harvest.

As a tri-part being, a Boss Chick takes care of her mind, body, and spirit. She fills her mind with intellect and yearns after wisdom and knowledge. She knows cleanliness is next to godliness, so she maintains her hygiene, and she makes it a priority to take measures to protect her health. Most importantly, a Boss Chick is led by her spirit. She follows that still small voice, which directs her in the way she should go. She maintains a relationship with God and takes time to worship Him, strengthening her connection. As a result, a Boss Chick is empowered and in touch with mind, body, and her spirit, and she lives with expectancy to receive her prize of eternal life. Therefore, under no circumstances does she compromise her self-worth for net worth! This virtuous quality certifies her as a Boss Chick!

PRACTICAL ANALYSIS

A lot of us start off on the right track in life, yet some where along the way we derail. Ever heard of the saying "more money, more problems?" It is so true! The more successful you become, the more enticing offers will be presented to you. Some of them will be legit, others will not. It is easier than you may think to fall in the trap of deception. After working so hard to rise to the top, many become greedy. The fear of not having, or losing out on something, has led to their demise.

A Boss Chick must not allow greed to destroy her empire. She protects herself by knowing "all money is not good money." Therefore, she carefully scrutinizes new opportunities and ensures they are not traps that can throw her off course. For she knows $1.00 today can potentially cost her $3.00 tomorrow, on top of unnecessary pain and hardship.

In this chapter, I will share a true story about a very good friend of mine, Jamila T. Davis, most of which is excerpted from her memoirs "She's All Caught Up" and "The High Price I Had To Pay." Her story is a cautionary tale which will broaden your scope and enlighten you to the severe consequences of compromising your self-worth for net-worth.

EXAMPLE ———

Jamila T. Davis was born in Queens, New York. Her mother Mrs. Davis was my 7th grade English teacher at J.H.S. 231 in Springfield Gardens, N.Y. Jamila grew up in a middle class area raised by both her parents. The Davises migrated to New York City from the South. They both grew up dirt poor and used education as a means to break the bonds of poverty. Having suffered numerous hardships themselves, the Davises were determined to provide their children with all the things they didn't have growing up.

As a result, both Jamila and her brother, Kee, were spoiled. Their parents bought them lots of nice things and kept them very active. It was Mrs. Davis's goal to ensure that her children were well-rounded. Jamila studied dancing, singing and acting, and she excelled. At the mere age of 12, she was recruited for a starring role in an off-Broadway play.

Not only did Jamila do well in the arts, she was also a straight A student. In her parents eyes they had raised their star child. Everything seem to go well with Jamila until she approached high school years. She was accepted to the acclaimed Fiorello LaGuardia High School of Performing Arts, also known as the "Fame" School of The Arts, where she was a drama major. Her new school required a commute using public transportation. Traveling required one bus and three trains. Jamila was so excited about her new independence and the ability to travel New York City freely. During her first week of school, she became enamored by a 16 year old boy, who was a big time drug dealer from 40 Housing Projects in South Jamaica Queens. The couple met at McDonalds, outside Parsons & Archer Train Station, after school.

For Jamila it was love at first sight! She was intrigued by her boyfriend's lifestyle. His money, flashy car and jewelry caught her attention, and his swag lured her in. A taste of life in the fast lane got her open, and she broke loose from her mother's tight reign. Consequently, she abandoned her goals and aspirations to be a star. Instead, she pursued the life of a hustler's wife.

From a young age, Jamila became consumed with materialism. She liked the attention that flashy cars, diamond jewelry and fur coats got her. Instead of building her self esteem by working on herself, she used material items to give her a false sense of worth. Driven by the "almighty dollar," she became a successful real estate broker and a lead-go-to person in the Hip-Hop music industry. Her fierce ambition also led her to open a financial services firm to bring in more revenue. Utilizing her knack for sales and marketing, overnight she became the talk of the music industry, and was sought out by big time hustlers who were attracted to the services she offered.

Jamila's businesses quickly took off, as she helped multitudes obtain luxury cars and procure the credit they needed to live the American dream. By the time she was 25 years old, Jamila became a multimillionaire who many celebrities depended on for financial management services. Jamila didn't just hoard her finances for herself. She shared her knowledge with many others, helping her peers obtain properties, set up businesses and become successful. She shared her wealth, as she made large contributions to churches and other civic organizations that she was involved with.

Although Jamila started off her companies on the right track, she received an offer that she couldn't refuse. A local mortgage broker offered her an opportunity to purchase several upscale homes in Alpine and Saddle River New Jersey. He had a hook up inside the bank who would get all the deals approved, no questions asked. Jamila knew the deals they put together would contain fraudulent financial information. But, she rationalized that since the mortgages would be paid on time and the bank would make money, taking the risk would be okay. In her mind, it was a "no harm, no foul" transaction that stood to gain her lots of money.

Giving it no second thought, Jamila arranged to close the deals and she made millions of dollars off the transactions. Her new wealth brought her even more recognition and prestige, escalating her into the world of professional sports players, who also became her clients.

Jamila had it all. By the age of 25, she controlled over $30 million dollars in real estate; she had a fleet of luxury cars, including a Bentley and a Maybach; and she had enough diamonds, furs and designer clothing to fill an entire store. Unfortunately, even with all the prestige, wealth and material items she chased after, she was still unhappy. Inside she felt empty, knowing there was something else she was missing. Material items could not fill this void.

With her new found money, came new problems. She had a crew of snakes surrounding her. But baby girl knew without a doubt, deep down none of them cared about her. They were users that merely desired her money. As long as she paid them well and they had access to the finer things in life, they stayed around, masking their true intentions. Little did Jamila know at the time, she would quickly get to see who was who.

The mortgage broker who financed Jamila's deals got into a jam. He did business with a woman that was on the police's radar, who Jamila had warned him to stay away from. Dismissing her advice, the mortgage broker closed two deals with this woman and caught the eyes of the FEDS. It all went down in flames after that! Jamila was charged and convicted of 7 counts of bank fraud. The mortgage broker, who Jamila helped to become a millionaire also, turned into a federal cooperator and testified against her.

On July 16, 2008, I had just became a proud mother, and my friend Jamila was sentenced to serve 12 1/2 years in prison for her participation in the crime. The mortgage broker who she got the hook up from was sentenced to 2 years in prison in exchange for his cooperation.

To date, Jamila has served close to 7 years behind bars. The cubicle she shares with a bunkie is smaller than the bread pantry in the home she once owned. Having to live out of a locker, smaller than the space under her bathroom sink, she realizes how her crime was not worth it. Abandoning her dreams and aspirations as a little girl, and compromising her integrity for what she perceived to be great success, cost her 12 1/2 years of her life!

Jamila's story represents a common trend in our society. Just like so many others, she thought the dark secrets of her past would never catch up with her. But they did, and at a time she least expected! When the FEDs came knocking, the majority of Jamila's so called friends vanished. I saw a movie, "The Great Gatsby," a few years ago, which reminds me of Jamila's present life. It troubles me that the character Gatsby's funeral service compares to her 12 1/2 year imprisonment. Where are her friends now?

Users will only remember the last thing you've done for them. You can give the people around you the world, but tough times reveal the character of those who are true and those who are fake. When users feel you're useless, they vanish into thin air, and they never look back!

Never think what you do in the dark won't come to light, especially if you become successful. Success breeds jealousy. Don't doubt for a second your confused admirers, who I call "haters", won't expose you, especially If they are given the opportunity. Be assured, they will take you down the first chance they get! Therefore, please protect yourself and your empire by not doing anything you'll later regret. Temporary gain is not worth a life time of sorrow, so here's a fair warning. Do not compromise your self-worth for net-worth or it could cost you a price you don't want to pay!

JEWEL DROPS

- A Boss Chick doesn't make plans to merely survive, she plans to leave behind a legacy that will last for many generations to come. In order to accomplish her goal, she knows she can not compromise her self-worth for net-worth, because that is a sure path to self-destruction.

- A Boss Chick knows she is a tri-part being, who was made in the image of her almighty Father. She is a spirit being, who lives in a body and possesses a soul. After her soul and body dies, her spirit lives on!
- A Boss Chick understands that through her spirit she is able to communicate directly to God. He speaks to her through a still voice that some refer to as intuition. Through her gut feelings she is led by Him, and she is protected.
- A Boss Chick knows distractions are used to blind and derail her, and the spirit of lust is used to lure her into sin. Therefore, she stays on top of her game and refuses to take the bait, because it will put her in a risk of forfeiting her divine destiny.
- A Boss Chick's body is her temple. It is a place where God resides. Knowing its value, she takes care of her body and does not defile it. No matter how rough times get, she never sells her body for temporary gain or pleasure. She stands firm on this principle! As a result, she is honored and respected!
- A Boss Chick refuses to be a slave to any man, job or organization. She does not let others make decisions for her, nor does she follow plans that may cause her potential harm. She is a free spirit who is led by God. Therefore, she refuses to allow people, places or things to become her jailor.

- A Boss Chick is a woman who pursues the path of a career versus a job. She knows a career will uplift her and lead her into her purpose, whereas a job is only a means to procure a paycheck. By pursuing her dreams, she finds the things she loves to do that will sustain her, give back to society and bring her joy. As a result, she is successful in her field of choice and she prospers!
- A Boss Chick is happy with the image she sees when she looks at her reflection in the mirror. She can walk the streets comfortably, without having to watch over her shoulder. She is a virtuous woman who feels good about herself and the choices she has made in life, so she is full of joy and confidence!
- As a tri-part being a Boss Chick takes care of her mind, body and spirit. She fills her mind with intellect and yearns after wisdom and knowledge. She knows that cleanliness is next to godliness, so she maintains her hygiene and she makes it a priority to take measures to protect her health.
- A Boss Chick is led by her spirit. She follows that still voice, which directs her in the way she should go. She maintains a relationship with God and takes time to worship Him, strengthening her connection. As a result, she is in touch with mind, body and spirit and she is empowered!

CHAPTER NINE

Commandment IX

"Thou Shall Not Keep What You Can't Trust, Nor Trust What You Can't Keep"

REVELATION

A Boss Chick is guided by the principle of loyalty. She is loyal to her family, friends, and those who work on her team. She does not backbite, degrade, or talk down to the individuals with whom her loyalty lies, nor does she allow others to mistreat them. A Boss Chick is known as a protector. She insulates those who she loves and cares about from gossip and unwanted degradation, becoming a shield that protects them from malicious attacks. As a result, she builds strong alliances with those around her who also extend their loyalty to her, creating a prosperous team.

A Boss Chick knows that trust is vital to building any productive relationship. Without it, a relationship has no foundation and cannot grow. A Boss Chick does not engage in relations with people who do not honor and value her, because she knows these individuals will not be loyal to her. Knowing that disloyal people are opportunists who will use her, abuse her, then kick her to the curb, she avoids all those who display disloyal characteristics.

A Boss Chick lives by the principle of loyalty. She carefully analyzes those whom she allows in her inner circle. She is not quick to call those whom she interacts with a friend, nor does she allow just anyone to become a part of her team. A Boss Chick is a woman who is watchful. She studies the character of the people who she deals with. She asks questions about their interests, and she looks for signs of suspicious behavior. Most importantly, she tests all those who she personally engages with to see if they are loyal. She may simply ask them to perform a task to see if the person really has her back. Or, she may divulge what appears to be sensitive information, to see if the person will disclose it to others. The results will determine if she can trust this person or not. A Boss Chick knows the best way for her to gain details about a new individual is to observe their long-term relationships with others. If a person is disloyal to those in their immediate circle, she takes it as a sign that this person will also be disloyal to her. If she can't trust the character of a person, she makes a conscious choice to let them go, which keeps her protected.

A Boss Chick does not place trust or confidence in people who do not deserve it. She doesn't base her relationships on what people say or intend to do. Instead, she lets their actions determine the basis of the relationship. When these individuals make a promise, she expects them to deliver, unless there is a very good excuse why they couldn't. She listens carefully to the words people share, but she does not categorize them as facts until she checks and verifies all important information for herself. Although a Boss Chick believes in giving everyone a second chance, she does not tolerate repeated excuses or abuse. When she sees a person doesn't live up to the standards she expects, she exits. Her exits are not brutal, cruel, or uncompassionate. Instead, she lovingly detaches herself and allows people to be who they are as she continues to strive and reach her goals in life. As a result, a Boss Chick only keeps like-minded people on her team, ones who share her same values and goals. They work harmoniously together, because they are cut from the same cloth!

A Boss Chick can spot a disloyal person two blocks up the street, because she knows the characteristics they possess. Disloyal people are masters of deception. They will lie, cheat, and steal to get what they desire. These individuals are selfish and can be heartless. They come around to get what they need, and then they leave. These are the type of individuals who will milk the cow until it is dry. They will even continue to come back until there is nothing left to take—then vanish.

Disloyal people will tell you everything you want to hear. They play on your emotions simply to get the things they desire. If you watch these individuals closely, you will notice their actions don't match up with their words. For instance, if a person tells you they love you, they will be concerned about your feelings and your needs. If they are constantly putting you down and taking away the things they know you need for yourself, they are disloyal.

Loyal people stand strong because they believe in who you are and the strength of the relationship that both of you have established. They do not just hang around for the good times; they are there to support you when times get rough. Loyal people do not kick you in the back when you are not looking. They honor you and protect you from others who wish to cause you harm. Loyal people are there to listen to you during your times of need. When you share secrets, they hold on to them, even to the grave. They are not people who slap you in the face with the information you shared, and they do not spread your business to others. Loyal people don't tear you down; they work hard to build you up. Loyal people are team players. They work harmoniously with you to achieve common dreams. They are the people you can count on to come to your rescue and help you fight battles you aren't strong enough to win on your own. They are dedicated soldiers in your life who are worth fighting for. When a Boss Chick recognizes loyal people on her team, she guards those relationships with her whole heart, because she appreciates their value!

A Boss Chick does not place a higher value on an individual than they deserve. She doesn't guess what their qualities and attributes consist of. She doesn't create false hope in individuals simply because she wishes they will measure up to her standards. A Boss Chick does not allow her judgments to become clouded by sexual favors, material items, or finances. Instead, she judges her potential alliances by the full scope of their interactions. She analyzes their actions and their motives, and she tests them to see if they are loyal. When their qualifications add up, she rightfully calls them her friends. Until then, she keeps these individuals as acquaintances.

A Boss Chick honors herself. Therefore, she refuses to be anyone's doormat. She does not let people walk over her or use her in the name of love or to gain acceptance. When she realizes people possess negative characteristics that can put her life in danger, she quickly lets them go. She does not keep company with liars, manipulators, deceivers, or opportunists. When she recognizes that people are in her life for the wrong reasons, she detaches! Sticking to this principle, a Boss Chick does not "keep what she can't trust, nor trust what she can't keep." As a result, she is protected and empowered!

PRACTICAL ANALYSIS

A Boss Chick knows if she trusts what she can't keep, it will cause her unnecessary pain and hardship. Taking heed to this principle, she chooses wisely those she will engage with. She does not intermingle in forbidden relationships that will violate her covenant protection with God; nor does she seek to engage with others who are in committed relationships with someone else, for she knows by violating this rule, she will open the doors to chaos and self-destruction. Therefore, she proceeds with caution and sets boundaries to protect her own well-being.

In this chapter, we will explore an example that illustrates the detriment of trusting what you can't keep. Take heed to this cautionary tale, as it displays multiple principles we've discussed in this book.

EXAMPLE ———

Carla and Andre Johnson were high school sweethearts who fell in love and got married after they completed college. Carla was a successful accountant, and Andre became a schoolteacher. The couple had two boys, who they raised in a nice suburban neighborhood.

Andre had aspirations of playing professional basketball. He was the star player on his high school team and landed a full scholarship to college; yet, he was unable to make it to the pros.

Andre trained both of his boys to excel in basketball. Day and night he would force them to practice. He even became the coach of their junior high basketball team. Although his boys were expected to maintain good grades, they had to live, eat, and sleep basketball. Carla felt her husband's behavior was a little obsessive, but she rationalized that he only wanted the best for his boys, so she supported him.

As a result of their extensive practice, both of their sons did extremely well in sports. Following their dad's lead, both boys became star players in school. The eldest son was so good he was drafted to the NBA straight out of high school as a number-one draft pick!

Andre was extremely happy about his son's success. Carla was excited too. It seemed as though the family was now complete as Andre lived vicariously through his son, yet life took a sudden twist in the Johnson household.

Upon his eldest son entering the NBA, Andre quit his job as a schoolteacher to go on the road and follow his son. Andre had the time of his life as he went from city to city, watching his child make major achievements in professional ball. Every victory his son achieved, Andre felt as he himself had won.

At first, Carla supported Andre's efforts. But as time went on, Andre stayed away from home for extended durations, and the couple began to lose their connection. Deep inside, Carla felt something was drastically wrong, yet she ignored her intuition and did not address her husband's behavior.

Andre felt like a college kid again, so he decided to relive his childhood dreams. Checking to see if he still had his swag, he began to flirt with Pattie, the head cheerleader on his son's team. Pattie had it going on! She was a smart girl with a lot of ambition, who was an aspiring actress. Pattie, who grew up without her father, gladly welcomed Andre's attention.

They spent lots of time together, and Andre inspired her in ways no other person had ever done. In his presence, she felt like she could conquer the world. His deep, passionate talks with her gave her fuel like never before!

Pattie knew Andre was married to Carla, so she was leery about engaging in a personal relationship with him. But, Andre convinced Pattie he was going to leave Carla, so she let her guard down and the two became a couple.

For many years Andre played a juggling act. He stayed at home with his wife for 2 weeks out of the month, and the other 2 weeks he stayed on the road with Pattie. Carla had no clue Andre was living a double life, and his son was too scared of his dad to get involved.

As time went on, Pattie began to question if Andre would ever leave Carla. Year after year, he made excuses as to why he had to stay, but assured her he would leave one day. Pattie, mesmerized by Andre, accepted his lies as the truth, even though deep down inside she felt he would never be hers. Although he knew he was being deceptive to Pattie, Andre trusted that she would remain true to him and follow all his instructions, which included staying away from his wife.

In an attempt to make Andre leave Carla, Pattie secretly got off of birth control and got pregnant. She felt with a new baby he would finally tell his wife the truth and leave her for good. She had no clue what chaos her news would bring!

When Pattie told Andre she was pregnant, she expected him to be excited, but he was far from happy. Andre felt Pattie had betrayed him, so instantly he flew into a rage. The thought he would finally have to tell Carla the truth made him sick inside. He really loved his wife and his family. He never had any intentions of getting caught up with Pattie. In his mind, he would just stick and move—but now he was stuck!

Thinking about the pain he would cause Carla and his family, he began to pull away from Pattie. After a few months he barely accepted any of her calls. Pattie was hurt at first, then her pain turned to anger. She was determined to make sure that Carla knew about her so she could break up their happy family.

Early one morning, Pattie decided to make an unexpected trip to Carla and Andre's home. After Andre found out Pattie was pregnant, he decided he would pour all his affection into his marriage. Having an epiphany of possibly losing his wife made him value all of her wonderful qualities. As a result, he began to pamper her, treat her well, and show her how much he loved and appreciated her. Carla was overjoyed; she felt like she had her old best friend back. Things finally seemed to be going well for the couple—until they got a knock on the door.

Andre's gut feeling led him to answer. He was shocked to see Pattie, who was 7 months pregnant with a full, round belly, standing on his porch.

"Honey, who is it?" Carla shouted from the hot tub where she was waiting for her husband to return.

"Oh, ah . . . nobody, honey. I believe this man has the wrong house," Andre shouted back. Thinking quick on his toes, he grabbed his pants and his .40-caliber gun from the drawer. Without thinking twice, Andre lured Pattie into his car and took her to the woods, where he shot her in the head three times. Leaving her lifeless body behind, he returned home as if nothing at all happened.

Several months went by, and he felt no remorse. In Andre's mind, the problem was finally fixed. He was relieved as he proceeded to move on with his life. All was well . . . until the past caught up with him. Pattie's body was eventually found and the DNA linked her back to Andre.

Today, Andre is serving a life sentence behind bars. Pattie is dead, and Carla had been confined to a mental health hospital. Each party in this love triangle experienced a tragic fate, all of which could have been avoided. Where did their relationships go wrong? And who trusted what they couldn't keep? This is the tragic fate of many who lie, cheat, and deceive in the name of love. Eventually, the past catches up to them, and all parties involved end up suffering. As a Boss Chick, you can protect yourself by not keeping what you can't trust, nor trusting what you can't keep, and by listening to your intuition. Take heed!

JEWEL DROPS

- A Boss Chick is guided by the principle of loyalty. She is loyal to her family, friends, and those who work on her team. She does not backbite, degrade, or talk down to the individuals with whom her loyalty lies, nor does she allow others to mistreat them.

- A Boss Chick is known as a protector. She insulates those whom she loves and cares about from gossip and unwanted degradation, becoming a shield that protects them from malicious attacks. As a result, she builds strong alliances with those around her who also extend their loyalty to her, creating a prosperous team.
- A Boss Chick carefully analyzes those whom she allows in her inner circle. She is not quick to call those whom she interacts with a friend, nor does she allow just anyone to become a part of her team. She studies the character of the people who she deals with and looks for signs of suspicious behavior. Most importantly, she tests the character of those she personally engages with to ensure they meet her standards.
- A Boss Chick knows the best way for her to gain details about a new individual is to observe their long-term relationships with others. If a person is disloyal to those in their immediate circle, she takes it as a sign that this person will also be disloyal to her.
- A Boss Chick does not place trust or confidence in people who do not deserve it. She doesn't base her relationships on what people say or intend to do. Instead, she lets her actions determine the basis of the relationship. When these individuals make a promise, she expects them to deliver, unless there is a very good excuse why they couldn't.
- Although a Boss Chick believes in giving everyone a second chance, she does not tolerate repeated excuses

or abuse. When she sees a person doesn't live up to the standards she expects, she exits. As a result, a Boss Chick only keeps like-minded people on her team. They work harmoniously together, because they are cut from the same cloth.

- A Boss Chick can spot a disloyal person two blocks up the street, because she knows the characteristics they possess. Disloyal people are masters of deception. They will lie, cheat, and steal to get what they desire. These individuals are selfish and can be heartless. They come around to get what they need until there is nothing left to take, then they vanish.
- Loyal people stand strong because they believe in who you are and the strength of the relationship that you both have established. They do not just hang around for the good times. They are there to support you when times get rough. They are the people you can count on to come to your rescue and help you fight battles you aren't strong enough to win on your own. They are dedicated soldiers in your life who are worth fighting for.
- A Boss Chick does not place a higher value on an individual than they deserve. She doesn't guess what their qualities and attributes consist of. She doesn't create false hope in individuals simply because she wishes they will measure up to her standards. Instead, she analyzes their actions and their motives, and she tests them to see if they are loyal.

- A Boss Chick honors herself. Therefore, she refuses to be anyone's doormat. She does not let people walk over her or use her in the name of love or to gain acceptance. When she realizes people possess negative characteristics that can put her life in danger, she quickly lets them go. She refuses to keep company with liars, manipulators, deceivers, or opportunists. Sticking to this principle, she is protected and empowered!

CHAPTER TEN

Commandment X

"Thou Shall be Leery Of The Company You Keep"

REVELATION

Ever heard of the saying "birds of a feather flock together"? Do you understand why this cliché is generally true? Over time, we become a reflection of those we are surrounded by. Subconsciously, we pick up habits, both good and bad, from those who we spend significant time with. Do you have a friend who often uses a certain saying or slang term and now you find yourself using it also? That's an example of how easily we pick up behaviors from others without actually realizing it. With that said, it is vital for a Boss Chick to be mindful of the company she keeps. If you hang out with lazy people who utilize deceptive measures to procure the things they want in life, they will eventually contaminate you with their "NMA." This acronym stands for Negative Mental Attitude. Even if it happens subtly, you will find yourself being drained of positive energy and "slow peddling" on the divine course for your life. Therefore, a Boss Chick is extremely selective of those whom she chooses to engage with.

Take a moment and analyze the people who are in your inner circle. Do you share like goals, morals, and tendencies? Do these individuals influence your choices in life? Do you admire the accomplishments of these individuals? Answering these questions will help you analyze the power of your relationships.

Everything you do in life requires faith. If you don't believe you can achieve success, you won't! In this case, it is your fear of flying that will prevent you from moving ahead. If you are an individual with little faith, if you hang out with others who don't believe in your dreams, you will eventually become spiritually crippled. The great achievers in the world have learned this secret: In order to fly, you need to surround yourself with eagles! They are individuals in your inner circle who are full of faith and energy, who believe in you and your dreams. These successful individuals will be there to catch you if you falter and will fuel you with inspiration so you can fly too! Having this wisdom, a Boss Chick surrounds herself with eagles. She knows that birds of a feather flock together, so she'd rather hang with eagles over pigeons, who will help her soar. When she notices individuals who are close to her don't share her faith and values, she quickly detaches. For she knows, those with contaminated faith can spoil her dreams and dampen her drive to push ahead.

A Boss Chick knows there are many energy thieves on the prowl, who come to take away, yet never choose to give. Therefore, she is watchful of those who always have a problem and often complain about their hardships. She realizes if she spends all her energy to comfort and uplift these individuals, she will not have the energy left to take care of herself. Therefore, she detaches as a means to guard herself from negativity.

A Boss Chick is a woman who is attracted to positive energy. Therefore, she seeks out individuals who share common goals, and she collaborates with them creating progressive movements. She is a businesswoman who dedicates time and energy networking. She is a member of several thriving organizations, social clubs, and business forums where she constantly meets new people who are able to assist in her pursuit of fulfilling her dreams.

A Boss Chick understands the characteristics of a true friend, so she is not easily fooled by imposters. She is cautious of those who do not have a backbone and who simply agree with whomever they hope to gain favor with. She is a strong woman who does not tolerate "yes-men" on her team. She knows true friends are honest individuals who will compliment her on her accomplishments, yet still constructively criticize when necessary.

A Boss Chick takes heed of individuals who try to clone her. She does not welcome those who choose to vicariously live through her, attempting to steal her style, ideas, and passion. For she knows by befriending covetous individuals who desire her lifestyle, it will fuel their jealousy. Every accomplishment she achieves will only cause them to lash out even more. To protect herself from unnecessary hardships she chooses to befriend individuals who are happy in their skin and content with their own accomplishments.

A Boss Chick is leery of those who find it hard to pay her a compliment, especially when called for; she knows that is a sure sign of jealousy! She rids herself of individuals who try their best to expose her flaws and have few positive things to say about her good qualities, because she knows these individuals do not wish her well.

A Boss Chick does not allow those who require handouts to enter her inner circle. She knows if she befriends the help, they will eventually become resentful and envious when they see the full scope of her lifestyle. Therefore, she makes friends with those on her level, who do not need her assistance. And she avoids making the maid into her houseguest, for she'll no longer clean, yet desire to take over the palace.

A Boss Chick does not jump at offers that seem too good to be true. She is not ruled by the "almighty dollar." Nor does she allow those with wrong intentions to enter her mix, in hopes of gaining wealth. Instead, she checks out all offers presented to her and does her due diligence to ensure she does not enter into risky relationships.

A Boss Chick is mindful to stay clear of those who delight in the misfortune of others. She realizes if they celebrate their neighbor's downfall today, chances are if she falls short, they will rejoice on her downfall tomorrow. Therefore, she inspects the character and intentions of those around her to ensure she keeps "haters" out of her camp!

A Boss Chick knows true friends care about what happens to her and they will protect her from harm. Therefore, her guard goes up when she notices those who are close to her don't take interest in her struggles or come to her defense. For a Boss Chick knows a real friend will never see her homeless, without a meal, or with no money; and a real friend will never walk away when she sees her hurting.

A Boss Chick monitors how her friends engage with her and others. She is a freehearted person, who goes hard for those she loves, yet she understands that for her friendships to work, they must be reciprocal. Therefore, she freely gives, yet she also allows room to receive. If she finds herself continuously giving and supporting her friends and they don't reciprocate or give back, it raises a red flag, and she proceeds with caution. If necessary, she tests those who are close to her to see where their heart is. As a result, if she finds out their intentions are no good, she quickly lets them go.

A Boss Chick knows from experience there is no use carrying garbage around. It will either cause her to stink, make her sick, or cause her to lose her positive energy.

Therefore, when a Boss Chick recognizes there is garbage in her camp, she immediately disposes of it! By doing so, she protects herself and stays free from contamination!

PRACTICAL ANALYSIS

Even the best of us can fall prey to bad company, as it is human nature to believe the intents of those we are around are pure. It isn't until we are crossed by those whom we love or trust the most that the real consequences for maintaining adverse relationships are illuminated.

In this chapter, I will use an example that illustrates how easily even a Boss Chick can fall victim to deception based on the company she keeps. Take heed to this example and protect yourself from those who do not have your best interest at heart!

EXAMPLE ———

Latesha was an aspiring actress who moved to Los Angeles from Detroit, Michigan. As a little girl she had dreams of Hollywood success, and she was determined to make it happen. Driving from Detroit to L.A., Latesha had $200 and a small suitcase with all the items she owned in her car. Although she had very little, her faith was very big! She believed God would align her with the right people, and He did!

While taking acting classes in Studio City, California, she met a rising television producer who she dated, named Rick.

He had great talent, yet he lacked the strong faith Latesha had. Recognizing his gift, Latesha fell in love with Rick and pushed him to achieve his dreams. Every time Rick experienced challenges, Latesha was right there to pick him up! She shared stories that her grandmother told her that helped inspire her to push ahead. Just as those stories attributed to increasing Latesha's faith, they did the same for Rick. As a result, Rick built the confidence he needed to pursue his dreams, and he captured them!

Rick became a successful Hollywood producer who won several awards for his productions. He didn't forget the ones who helped him achieve his victory. Latesha stood right by his side the whole way through, and Rick returned the favor by casting her in his first movie.

From the moment the movie aired, Latesha's career took off! Her appearance gained her recognition and several parts in other productions. The couple was finally living their dreams, and they had the company of each other to share their journey to the top.

One day Latesha got a phone call from her friend Renee from back home. Just like Latesha, Renee aspired to be an actress, but she didn't have the knowledge or resources to make her dream a reality. Renee asked Latesha if she could move in with her and Rick until she got on her feet and landed her first job. Latesha didn't think twice before saying yes. She was happy to help her old friend achieve her dreams too.

Renee took a flight to Los Angeles with only the clothes on her back, and Latesha welcomed her with open arms. The first thing Renee noticed was the beautiful house on the hills the couple lived in. Latesha was well established and lived a luxurious lifestyle, far different from her life back in Detroit. She had all the things Renee desired. For hours, Renee got lost imagining that Latesha's life was her own. She felt as if Latesha was her equal, so if she could make it, Renee could make it too.

As time went on and Latesha made her comfortable, Renee began to believe she deserved to live the wonderful life that Latesha extended to her. As a result, her attitude changed. She was no longer humble or grateful; instead, she became rude and obnoxious.

Renee made Latesha's castle her home. She began to rearrange the furniture and even wear Latesha's clothes without her permission. Latesha didn't pay Renee's behavior too much attention at first. She felt the least she could do was give back to someone in need, as God had blessed her greatly.

In the beginning, Rick couldn't stand Renee. In his heart, he felt she was an opportunist, but he couldn't convince Latesha otherwise, so he let it go. While Latesha was out working, Renee began to take care of Rick. She cleaned his clothes, ironed, and even cooked for the couple, which Latesha appreciated. She simply felt her friend was earning her keep. Renee's hospitality gained Rick's attention. He was even inclined to recruit Renee for his next film. As Rick became friendlier to her, she spruced up her image, attempting to gain his affection.

One late afternoon, Rick woke up to the warm sensation of hands rubbing on his leg. Smelling his wife's sweet perfume he rolled over to make love to her. As he entered into her sweet chamber he noticed there was something different about his experience, yet he brushed it off.

"Oh, Rick, I always longed for us to be together. Latesha doesn't deserve you. All she thinks about is her career. It's me who loves you. I am the one," Renee moaned—and Rick jumped back.

Renee was dressed in Latesha's lingerie, coated in Latesha's perfume, and wore her hair like her as well. Although Rick was mortified to know he was deceived by Renee, the thrill of her seduction did not die off right away.

"Rick, it's okay. I know you want me. I can give you something Latesha could never give you. Take a look at all of this," Renee said seductively as she twirled in front of him with her naked body provocatively.

Rick and Renee passionately made love again. Lost in the moment they both were unaware Latesha had entered the room. Latesha's mouth dropped as she watched her man making passionate love to her friend. Without thinking, Latesha jumped on the bed and began to fight both Rick and Renee. Rage ran through her entire body as she felt betrayed by the two people she loved the most.

That same night Renee was kicked out on the streets. Forced to return to Detroit with no money, she lost out on her opportunity to become an actress. Latesha refused to give Rick another chance, so the couple broke up and parted ways. Although Latesha is still doing very well as an actress, she has not dated another man since. She now has trust issues that block her from intimacy. She doesn't believe she'll ever be able to love again.

SUMMATION

Latesha's tragic fate could have been prevented had she been leery of the company she kept. All the signs were there, but she refused to take notice. She was naive and gullible, which made her easy prey for Renee.

Boss Chicks, there will always be "telltale" signs, so take heed! Do not let people in your inner circle who do not honor, respect, and show you love. When you notice someone is jealous of you or desires what you have, break loose from them! If not, it can cost you your happiness!

JEWEL DROPS

- A Boss Chick surrounds herself with eagles. She understands that birds of a feather flock together, so she'd rather hang with eagles over pigeons, because she knows they will help her to soar.
- A Boss Chick knows there are many energy thieves on the prowl who come to take away, yet will never choose to give. Therefore, she is watchful of those who always have a problem and often complain about their hardships. She realizes if she spends all her energy to comfort and

uplift these individuals, she will not have energy left to take care of herself. Therefore, she detaches as a means to guard herself from negativity.

- A Boss Chick is a woman who is attached to positive energy. Therefore, she seeks out individuals who share common goals, and she collaborates with them creating positive moments. She is a businesswoman who dedicates time and energy networking. She is a member of several thriving organizations, social clubs, and business forums where she constantly meets new people who are able to assist in her pursuit to fulfill her dreams.
- A Boss Chick understands the characteristics of a true friend, so she is not easily fooled by imposters. She is cautious of those who do not have a backbone and simply agree with whomever they desire to gain favor with. She is a strong woman who does not tolerate "yes-men" on her team. For she knows true friends are honest individuals who compliment her on accomplishments, yet still constructively criticize when necessary.
- A Boss Chick takes heed of individuals who try to clone her. She does not welcome those who choose to vicariously live through her, attempting to steal her style, ideas, and passion. For she knows by befriending covetous individuals who desire her lifestyle, it will fuel their jealousy. To protect herself from unnecessary hardships, she chooses to befriend individuals who are happy in their skin and content with their own accomplishments.

- A Boss Chick is leery of those who find it hard to pay her a compliment, especially when called for; she is a wise woman who knows this is a sure sign of jealousy! She rids herself of individuals who try their best to expose her flaws and have few positive things to say about her good qualities, because she knows these individuals do not wish her well.
- A Boss Chick does not allow those who require handouts to enter her inner circle. For she knows if she befriends the help, they will eventually become resentful and envious when they see the full scope of her lifestyle. Therefore, she makes friends with those on her level, who do not need her assistance. And, she avoids making the maid into her houseguest, for she'll no longer clean, yet desire to take over the palace.
- A Boss Chick does not jump at offers that seem too good to be true. She is not ruled by the "almighty dollar." Nor does she allow those with wrong intentions to enter her mix, in hopes of gaining wealth. Instead, she checks out all offers presented, and she does her due diligence to ensure she does not enter in risky relationships.
- A Boss Chick is mindful to stay clear of those who delight in the misfortune of others. She realizes if they celebrate their neighbor's downfall today, chances are if she falls short, they will rejoice on her downfall tomorrow. Therefore, she inspects the character and intentions of those around her to ensure she keeps "haters" out of her camp!

- A Boss Chick knows true friends care about what happens to her and they protect her from harm. Therefore, her guard goes up when she notices those who are close to her don't take interest in her struggles or come to her defense. For a Boss Chick knows a real friend will never see them homeless, without a meal, or with no money; and a real friend will never walk away when she sees her hurting.

EPILOGUE

"E, you hit a pothole. Watch the road, homie!" I said, annoyed I was awaken out of my sleep.

"My bad, Ma. Damn! We're only in P.A.? I got to get a few things. Do you mind if I stop at the mall?" he asked as we approached a huge shopping center.

"Handle your handle. I'm straight, you paid me. Do what you need to do and let's get you upstate to your family," I replied.

As I looked up and saw a sign that read I-84, E pulled into the shopping center and parked near a Petland store. Approximately 10 minutes later he came back to the car with bags of pet food.

"E, we stopped for freaking pet food?" I questioned, displaying my frustration.

"My daughter has a dog. I promised her I'd get him some food," he replied.

"I'm driving now! My liquor has worn off, so where do you need to go now?" I asked as I crossed over to the driver's seat, anxious to end the trip.

"Target, Marshalls, and Macy's, if you don't mind, Sunny," he replied pleasantly.

I took E to Target and Marshalls. Then, I drove over to Macy's department store and found a good parking spot in the cut, so I could take a quick nap. As I finally started to relax the sun began to beam brighter and brighter, and I became uncomfortable. I don't know what was more annoying, the sun or the mall security officer's vehicle, which kept circling around my car.

Approximately 15 minutes had passed, yet it seemed more like half an hour, and I became agitated. E had still not returned. I called his cell phone to see what was taking him so long. His phone rang four times and went to his voice mail. I called back, and it did the same thing. As I waited for E to return, I took notice of an envelope full of money that sat beside his Yankee fitted cap and his white T-shirt on the passenger side of the floor. I put the envelope in my Louis Vuitton bag as a security precaution, and then I proceeded to exit my vehicle. Before I could open my door, a police officer knocked on my window. I quickly cut my car back on and rolled down my window to see what he wanted.

"Ma'am, I'm going to need to detain you!" the police officer announced.

"Excuse me, sir. Detain me for what?" I questioned, alarmed by his presence.

"Are you here alone?" the officer asked.

"No, I am not," I replied quickly.

"I need your license and registration, please," the officer demanded, and I honored his request.

"Do you know a gentleman by the name of Eric?" the officer further questioned.

"No, I don't, Officer," I replied, quick on my toes, realizing Eric may have gotten into trouble. I was afraid at this point my association with him had put me in harm's way. But my curiosity got the best of me.

"Why are you asking me questions about someone named Eric? Is he OK?" I asked the officer nonchalantly.

"No, he's not. Eric's cell phone was confiscated, and he has missed calls from a 'Sunny Money.' I'm going to detain you and put you into handcuffs until we straighten this out. Can I check your vehicle?" he asked as he proceeded to open my car door and escorted me out of the vehicle.

"Absolutely not!" I yelled and grabbed my cell phone before I exited the car. "Get a warrant, and while I am being detained I want to speak to your boss!" I said angrily in defense.

I left my belongings in my car and was escorted in handcuffs through Macy's department store to a small dark room. Shortly after I was detained, a man with a black jacket, bearing the words FBI peeked in and snapped a picture of me. Immediately I realized whatever Eric had done was serious, and I became frantic!

"Sir, please, let me go! I have nothing to do with Eric. I want to go home, Officer. Please let me go! I didn't do anything!" I cried profusely.

"Sunshine, when you told me you didn't know Eric, it gave me probable cause to detain you. Furthermore, his call log shows you called him several times, which matches the cell phone we just apprehended from you," the officer said.

"So what does that have to do with arresting me? I'm in law school, sir. I know my rights! I want my lawyer and a phone call now!" I said frantically as an attempt to defend myself from being arrested.

"Sunshine, you are being placed under arrest because Eric, who is now being detained too, was trafficking counterfeit $100 bills in Target and Petland. We watched him go from store to store to buy various items. But we had no idea what car he drove." I listened intently to his words, and when I processed what he said I lost it!

"Counterfeit money? Oh no!!!" I cried realizing that E had me all hemmed up.

"Well, you are his partner, right?" the officer asked.

"What the hell are you talking about? Eric paid me $1,000 for the inconvenience to drive him upstate. All I did was assist him in the solution to his crisis. It is not a crime to give your friend a ride to meet with his daughter's mother and his child, right?"

"Well, we got that warrant you requested and in your bag we recovered $4,500 worth of counterfeit $100 bills," the officer said nonchalantly as he appeared to disbelieve my story.

"Huh? I only put his money in my pocketbook because he left it on the floor of my car. I was headed to Macy's when he didn't answer his cell. The other $1000 in my wallet is what he paid me as taxi fare to drive him upstate. I'm a businesswoman, sir. I don't need anything counterfeit. I am insulted!" I replied furiously.

The officer instructed me to stand up and follow another officer to make the phone call I requested. I called my mother-in-law at her home and instructed her to get in contact with my husband, who was out of town on business. I let her know I was being placed under arrest in Scranton, Pennsylvania, and asked her to pick up my son from day care. With only one allowed call, I knew she could relay the message and ensure my son got home safely from school. With no hesitation or questions she agreed to do both, which put my mind a little more at ease.

"OK, Ms. Smith, here's your arrest paperwork. It's time for you to see the judge now," the officer said.

With nothing but a prayer and unanswered questions, I sat there and cried to God, asking Him for clarity and help. I stood before the magistrate and my bail was set at $200,000. I looked down, and my life flashed before my eyes. All my hard work and achievements went out the window, including my education that took me many years to obtain. With an arrest I knew all my certifications and licenses I procured would be taken away, and I'd be right back at step one, the housing projects. The thought made me vomit. As I waddled in grief, I saw my son's face flash before my eyes, the disappointment from my grandmother and mother, and the look of happiness from the haters who never wanted me to succeed. My heart started pulsating, and I felt extremely light-headed. At that very moment I felt like giving up!

The officer took me back into the police vehicle, and then he looked in his rearview mirror with disappointment.

"Where am I being taken to now?" I asked as tears rolled down my eyes.

"I'm dropping you off at a holding cell until an officer comes to pick you up. He or she will take you to Lackawanna County Prison where you are going to be housed," he replied as he stared in my eyes. "Can I ask you a question, Ms. Smith?"

"Yes sir," I replied humbly feeling extremely remorseful.

"You had business cards in the bag we retained from your vehicle. We profiled you, and I know you are very successful and educated. Why would you even hang out with a guy like this?" the officer questioned.

"I have no idea," I said as I shook my head in disappointment, and we arrived back at the precinct.

"Hold on to your arrest documents. Your cuffs will be removed once I drop you off at the holding cell. If you have learned anything today, I hope it was to be more mindful of the company you keep!"

AFTERWORD

Sunny 101: The 10 Commandments of a Boss Chick was written on top of my bunk bed in a room I shared with five other roommates at the Danbury Federal Prison Camp, in Danbury, Connecticut. After serving time in Lackawanna County Prison and several months after being bonded and released to a federal ankle bracelet with a curfew, I was sentenced to an additional 4 months in prison. In September 2014, instead of starting fall classes to obtain my master's degree in business, I had to withdraw from college to prepare myself mentally, emotionally, and financially to go back to prison to serve my sentence for Conspiracy to Negotiate Counterfeit Money, based on my association with Eric, who I opted to give a ride to. Being caught up in the wrong place, at the wrong time, with the wrong individual, has not only caused me pain, hardships, and embarrassment, it also cost me time away from my loved ones!

As I reflect back on my mistakes and evaluate my life, I realize that even the best of us can get caught up! After spending hours with my friend Jamila T. Davis, whose story I share in this book, I realize how valuable a tool like my book can be to prevent other women from making the same mistakes we did.

Most importantly, I'm writing this book to encourage all women, no matter how old or young you are, to push ahead! Don't focus on how big your problems may seem. Instead, focus on how big your God is! He has personally proven Himself to me!

I thought imprisonment would be the worst experience in my life, but God has turned my journey around and used it for my good. I always wanted to write a book, but with my busy schedule I never had the time. My stay behind bars has given me a well-needed period to focus, reanalyze my life, and acknowledge my shortcomings, which I openly share with you.

As you see, I am not perfect, but my experience has taught me many valuable lessons that will benefit me greatly in the future. Together, my hope is that we can dust ourselves off and achieve our dreams, despite the bumps in the road along our path.

A Boss Chick is not a woman who claims to never make mistakes. She is a woman who learns from her past and utilizes her challenges to become a better person. She is a courageous woman that can see opportunity even in her worst circumstances and take advantage of them. Although she may get knocked down at times by the fierce obstacles of life, you can count on a Boss Chick to get up and rise above adversity!

Once again, my fellow Boss Chicks, I am Sunshine Smith-Williams, a woman who has experienced many obstacles in my life, yet I strive to continuously overcome them all! It is my experience and the lessons I've learned in the wilderness that make me an ultimate Boss Chick extraordinaire. The same can happen for you!

Best Wishes,
Sunshine Smith-Williams

ABOUT THE AUTHOR

Sunshine Smith-Williams was raised in Queens, New York by her mother, who struggled to make ends meet, in the absence of her dad. Smith-Williams grew up in impoverished housing projects with dim hope. Utilizing education as a weapon to overcome poverty, she obtained several degrees and certifications, climbing the corporate ladder to achieve success. After being laid off from her dream job in 2010, Smith-Williams gained the faith to start her own business. Through an intense journey that equipped her to discover her gifts and talents, dethrone her character flaws and increase her self-esteem, she successfully opened several thriving businesses and mentored others to do the same. This experience enlightened Smith-Williams to her purpose. Her life is a living testament that the past, regardless of the mistakes you make or your background, does not have to dictate your future! She shares this message of hope with both youth and adults across the world, inspiring them to overcome life's difficulties. Smith-Williams currently resides in Nassau County, New York with her husband, who is also her business partner, and their six year old son.

ORDER FORM

Mail to: 196-03 Linden Blvd.
St. Albans, NY 11412
or visit us on the web @
www.vocseries.com

QTY	Title	Price
	The High Price I Had To Pay	7.99
	The High Price I Had To Pay 2	7.99
	The High Price I Had To Pay 3	9.99
	She's All Caught Up	15.00
	How To Navigate Through Federal Prison And Gain An Early Release	39.95
	Sunny 101: The 10 Commandments Of A Boss Chick	14.95
	Total For Books	
	20% Inmate Discount -	
	Shipping/Handling +	
	Total Cost	

* Shipping/Handling 1-3 books 4.95
4-9 books 8.95

* Incarcerated individuals receive a 20% discount on each book purchase.

* Forms of Accepted Payments: Certified Checks, Institutional Checks and Money Orders.

* Bulk rates are available upon requests for orders of 10 books or more.

* Curriculum Guides are available for group sessions.

* All mail-in orders take 5-7 business days to be delivered. For prison orders, please allow up to (3) three weeks for delivery.

SHIP TO:
Name: ______________________
Address: ______________________

____

____

City: ______________________

State: ______________________ Zip: __________

Made in the USA
San Bernardino, CA
02 February 2020